TEXAS RANGER LEO BISHOP

HIS LEGENDARY LIFE AND TIMES...
A PERSONAL GLIMPSE

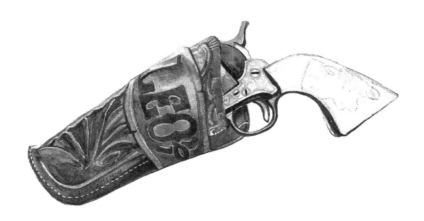

BY

BETTY OGLESBEE

ILLUSTRATIONS BY

KIM WHITTON

Paperback ISBN 978-1-68179-349-8
Hardback ISBN 978-1-68179-264-4

Printed in the United States

INTRODUCTION

Well documented, widely published accounts of the dangerous and turbulent times existing in the historic East Texas community of San Augustine during the mid-1930s and following years are available from a number of sources for those seeking more information related to the fateful events of that time. Our purpose, in the 1919 San Augustine County Jail Restoration Project, was to provide a quite broader picture using a positive approach, as we celebrated the lives of Alcaldes, Texas Rangers, Sheriffs, Game Wardens, Highway Patrol, Justices of the Peace, Constables, Judges, City Police…i.e., all aspects of law enforcement and its considerable history relating to our county's special place in the Deep East Texas Area.

We approached the San Augustine County Commissioners Court with confidence, since our San Augustine Garden Club had successfully prepared, funded, and submitted master plans/grant applications to the Texas Historical Commission to restore/preserve the 1927 San Augustine County Courthouse, rededicated in November 2010. Certainly the pitiful, moldy, stucco-covered 1919 jail, located on the historic 1833 Courthouse Square right next to the freshly restored courthouse, deserved attention. The idea of the 1919 county jail, repurposed as a Law Enforcement Museum and Texana Library, appealed to the judge and commissioners, and we were advised to proceed, with haste!

Anything related to law enforcement in the history of San Augustine was researched by genealogy professionals Connie Owens and Suzanne Sowell, who also categorized and arranged the Texana Library collection of Willie Earl Tindall, wife of longtime Sheriff Nathan Tindall, in a converted jail cell reading room, or "research cubby." Nancy and Karen Mills compiled the *San Augustine Tribune* records relating to Sheriff Nathan Tindall.

San Augustine Public Library's Frances Burks provided valuable information relating to Leo Bishop and the Texas Rangers from the early *San Augustine Tribune* records during the years 1935-1939. Historian Neal Murphy and County Clerk Margo Noble provided valuable documentation from the indexed and digitized county records, many dating long before Texas Independence. Multiple donations of law enforcement memorabilia came from relatives and friends of current and former county officials. Original keys to the 1919 jail cells were found and contributed by Sheriff Robert Cartwright. Surprisingly, they still work! The restored jail was re-dedicated on March 2, 2018.

San Augustine County Law Enforcement Museum & Texana Library

The 1927 San Augustine County Courthouse was restored with an 85/15 Courthouse Preservation Grant from the Texas Historical Commission, through the funding efforts of San Augustine Garden Club. The building was rededicated in November 2010.

During the process of fundraising for the jail restoration project, we heard of an upcoming estate sale to be conducted in the Rayburn Country locale by "Junktique" of Jasper, Texas for the estate of Bettye Bishop Robbins, daughter of Texas Ranger Leo Bishop. We spoke with owner Theresa Belew, who explained that the sale would include a large box of memorabilia relating to Bettye's father, Texas Ranger Leo Bishop. We learned that Bettye was not only an accomplished artist and writer for frequent articles in the *Jasper Newsboy*, but had been the historian of the Bishop family as well. Julia Wade, Mollie Litton, and I decided that under no circumstances could we miss going to this might-be-important estate sale. Julia's husband Nelsyn Wade had graduated from San Augustine High School in 1939 with classmate Carolyn Bishop, Leo's eldest daughter.

On the foggy spring morning of the sale, we traveled down Highway 96 at the crack of dawn in order to arrive well before the 7:00 a.m. opening. With hardly a car in sight during the 45-minute drive, we turned into the Rayburn Country sub-division to find all sides of the streets lined with cars for blocks, and scores of people waiting outside with anticipation for the appointed moment.

As promised, Theresa had "set aside" the box of Leo Bishop memorabilia for us to see before anyone else. She directed us to Bettye's studio, a small upstairs room filled with beautiful oil paintings, her easel and paints still in view, as if she had just left the room for a cup of coffee, and would be back soon. We immediately claimed this quite interesting box full of papers, documents, photos, interviews, and citations. Suddenly, we noticed a beautiful painting, very different from the lovely fruit, flower, and landscape subjects so prominently displayed throughout the room. It was on the floor, leaned against the wall, an oil painting with a familiar look…a scene from San Augustine that the three of us recognized at once. It was the old Stephenson house, directly across from the Memorial Medical Center, on the corner of Hospital and Milam streets. The Bishop family had purchased the home and lived there during their three-year stay in San Augustine. In the picture, with the house in the background, were two young girls playing "jacks"…Leo's daughters Carolyn and Bettye. On the right was a black Texas Ranger car, with Ranger Leo Bishop standing beside it. Fortunately, Theresa allowed us to purchase the painting for a reasonable sum. The picture is now on display in the 1919 San Augustine County Jail Museum, for the enjoyment of all.

Also visiting the Bettye Bishop Robbins estate sale that day was artist extraordinaire Kim Whitton, who purchased a voluminous generational collection of Bishop family photos and information. The combination of our two collections became the inspiration for this work. Kim's artistic talents and perceptive discernment in capturing the personalities of her subjects are a delightful addition to the narratives and documentation relating to Texas Ranger Leo Bishop's life and times.

Betty Oglesbee

Home of The Leo Bishop family at the corner of Milam and Hospital Streets in San Augustine, Texas. The Bishop family purchased this home early in their three-year stay in San Augustine, and owned the property until 1947.

Original Oil painting by Bettye Bishop Robbins

PICTOURGRAPH 508—OFFICERS WOOD (LEFT) AND ASH (RIGHT) MEXICAN BORDER CUSTOMS LINE RIDERS 35 YEARS AGO BEFORE THE TIME OF THE AUTOMOBILE., ALL SUPPLIES WERE CARRIED ON MULES TRAINED TO FOLLOW LIKE DOGS. BOTH MEN ARE OLD COWBOYS, WERE TWO OF COL. THEO. ROOSEVELT'S BRONCHO TWISTERS AND EX-ROUGH RIDERS. BROWN HORSE (RIGHT) RAISED BY PAT GARRETT, FAMOUS NEW MEXICO SHERIFF. MR. ASH IS A POLICE OFFICER IN EL PASO, TEXAS, AT THE PRESENT TIME. PHOTO COPYRIGHT—1938 BY A. C. ASH.

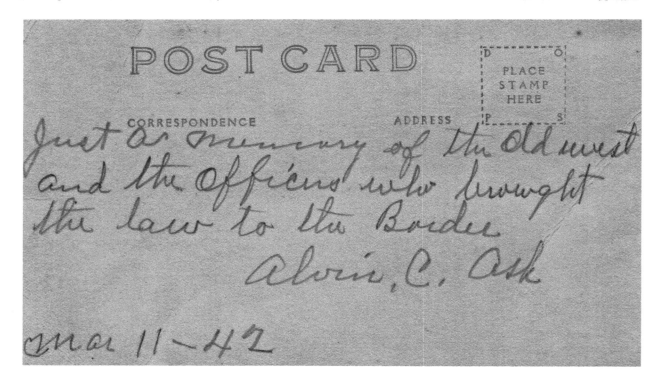

Postcard given to Ranger Leo Bishop from his friend Alvin C. Ash

AN INTERVIEW WITH TEXAS RANGER LEO BISHOP

Dr. Ben Proctor interviewed Leo Bishop on September 12,1968 at his home in Carta Valley, Texas. Dr. Proctor's *JUST ONE RIOT*, *Episodes of Texas Rangers in the 20th Century*, published in 1991 by Eakin Press, Austin, Texas, included a chapter entitled *"Leo Bishop and the San Augustine Crime Wave"*

The following narrative is edited from thirty-nine pages of transcribed Dictabelt Interview Tapes contained in the Bishop family papers. Suggestion: read Leo's answers "out loud" for an appreciation of his vernacular.

SELECTED EXCERPTS

Interviewer: I've heard a number of people say that the Rio Grande Valley and the border is a completely different world than the East Texas area. So first, tell us about informers...is there any special way you handle these people...any special techniques?

BISHOP: There's no special technique that I know of. It's just that you've got to talk their language, like the Mexicans, 'cause very few of them talk English, and you want them to understand about legal matters or some violation that's been committed. I've heard a lot of old time peace officers that had worked in different parts of the State of Texas that expressed my views exactly about the difference in the way you had to operate as a peace officer along the Mexican border as compared to North Texas or East Texas or something...just a different kind of people that you worked with and you had to use different tactics to get the job done in different parts of the state.

Interviewer: And sometimes people in different parts of the state don't understand this?

BISHOP: Oh yes, you run into that everywhere. They don't understand. In other words, when I went to San Augustine in East Texas I thought it was the toughest place I ever got into in my life. I carried a rifle and two six shooters on the streets of that little ole town around there for two or three months just to keep some son-of-a-gun from shooting me in the back off the top of one of them buildings or from behind a log or something because I knew they'd do it. That was the tactics they used over there. And still them people over there, the people that I talked to and the good people there, they thought that because I was from the Mexican border that I'm bound to be a tough son-of-a-gun 'cause they thought the Mexican border was the toughest place in the world. Well, there had been a lot of good peace officers killed up and down this border, but there had been a lot of good people as well as peace officers killed right over there in East Texas...several Texas Rangers ambushed and killed. That's the kind of stuff they did over there, there wasn't any fair fight to them. (I soon learned) you could just bluff them people over there plum out of town, which I did. When I went in there I couldn't get the good people to talk to me, because they were afraid some of them kinfolks of theirs was looking at 'em and would kill 'em that night in bed. (I decided I could) bluff all them outlaws, which I did. I hunted them up and called them everything I could think of and told 'em what I knew about 'em, and told 'em the damn county wasn't big enough for me and them both and they'd leave, they'd go plum to Louisiana and one ole outlaw, finally sent to the electric chair. He left and went to Louisiana for two or three months when I challenged him, and of course I couldn't arrest him because I couldn't get any evidence against him, and as long as he was lookin', why nobody else would tell me anything. But when I run him off and he left the county and everybody decided he was gone for awhile, then it took two or three stenographers to take down the stuff people knew about him. And finally he was scared so doggone bad he run and run and run and laid out a night and fought mosquitoes in them woods over there and them swamps in Louisiana. Finally (he) came into the sheriff's office in Beaumont, Texas and the sheriff was old Bill Richardson, great big fellow, a good friend of mine, and he told Bill and said, "That damn Ranger up there at San Augustine is huntin' me and I know he's gonna kill me. I've just run for a month or two here to kinda stay away from him. I want to turn myself in to you, for you to put me in your jail to protect me." Hell, I hadn't run him nowhere, just told him to leave the county and he did. Told him what I knew about him and told him if I caught him on the street again, he'd better be armed because I was gonna come a shootin'. And he believed it every bit. I just run him out of town so I could get information and send him to the electric chair. Well, he was finally brought to trial.

Interviewer: A lot of people in the State of Texas know about the Texas Rangers, particularly in the period when you worked. But, most of the previous history of the Texas Rangers was in the Border Country and so throughout the first hundred years.

BISHOP: Fighting Indians and Mexicans mostly and cow thieves. Yeah.

Interviewer: Do you think it was also part of the bigness of the area, you know, like not many people, or a lot of distance between… (it being) really wide open country, where you can't really control it too much?

BISHOP: Right. It's been that way a long time, you know, and that's where the Rangers originally built their reputation as good peace officers and fighting men, because they worked it first, and it was the "baby" of a foreign country where the Mexicans still "remembered the Alamo" and every time they came over here it was trouble. I worked with the mounted U.S. Customs a lot of times, and most of them were old ex-Texas Rangers.

Interviewer: (Back to the original question)...Is the usual term you hear "stool pigeon"...but what terms in particular did you use and when?

BISHOP: We called them informers. Any good officer has got to have an underground connection if he gets any information. And, of course, that's one of the first things I'd do anyplace I went to, is try to find somebody who had connections with the outlaw element that would...knew about it when I wanted to know something. Well, East Texas has a large population of negroes. And some of the best citizens I ever saw were black. Their wives kept a good, clean house and they were just as honest and hard working as could be, and I could ask them anything and swore it was the truth...I knew it was the truth when I heard it, too. There was a few of them kind over there I could trust.

Interviewer: Tell me about Ranger Bob Goss...he's got a reputation for being an awful fine shot. You do too, don't you?

BISHOP: Well, no, I wasn't quite as good as Bob. All my shootin' was done without pointin' my finger. I still shoot a rifle the same way. If I jump a deer out of one of these canyons out here and he comes tearin' out of the brush I never do aim at him. I just shoot from my hip. I kill 'em a runnin' just as fast as they can run just that way. I shot a six-shooter the same way. Whenever I pulled my pistol I just shot it, you know. If I went out on a firin' range and tried to shoot at a bulls eye I couldn't hit the board it was on, just trying to hold my gun still and aimin' at it. That was just something you acquired by practice, of course, you might say. I killed buzzards flying with a 32-20 rifle before I shot up the first box of cartridges by the time I was nine years old. You know, things like that I can't explain. I was just born and raised out on the ranch with my Dad, and I was the oldest one of his boys and he trained me from the start…I don't even remember the first time I ever shot a gun. And I rode horseback and followed him over the range when I was four years old. And I just grew up with those kind of things, and I don't know how I learned to shoot or how I learned to do a lot of things. But anyway, they came in handy when I got to be a pistol packer and had to do it for a living to school my kids and feed my wife. Why, things like that was one reason they chose me in the Ranger Service. I'm sure they learned those things about me before they took me in the Ranger Service. And Bill Sterling told me one time that he investigated me before they appointed me and found out that I had all the requirements that they wanted for a good Texas Ranger, and he thought I was one of the best after I'd been in there only a year or so.

Interviewer: What did you really think of Bill Sterling as the Adjutant General and of course, he was head of the Texas Rangers, but as an Adjutant General?

BISHOP: He was a wonderful guy. He promoted our service and brought it up out of the mud where it had been drug in the mud as a political football for a long time. And, of course, it was still a political football when I first got in there, proof of that was the way (Governor) Ma Ferguson kicked it plum out of the park when she was elected over ole man Ross Sterling. In the only time in the history of Texas, she fired every man on the payroll.

Interviewer: What about Bob Goss?

BISHOP: Bob was a good officer. And a well-respected officer. And a good fellow to be with.

Interviewer: Let's talk about your time in San Augustine…when you first went there, what the difficulties were.

BISHOP: When they sent us over there (Texas Rangers McCormick, Hines, and Bishop) Governor James Allred has just been inaugurated the day before. Edward Clark, his personal secretary, grew up in San Augustine and his mother and dad and his brother and sisters all still lived there. And, of course he told the governor first hand all this stuff that had been going on. Well, under Ma Ferguson the past two years, every thug in that county had a "Special Ranger Commission" and they was robbing, raping, and killing and more murders in that town…and there had never been a man indicted for it a'tall. People who lived there all their lives saw this happening every day. When Governor Allred sent me and those two other guys to San Augustine there was three of "Ma's" Rangers there. We had a letter of dismissal to them when we got there and presented it to their captain, a great big Swede. They all left town that night and we took charge. There was twenty-eight of Ma Ferguson Special Ranger Commissions in that little town. These thugs was wearing pistols around there. And a man comes to town with a bale of cotton, and sells it and starts to the bank to cash his check, there'd be two or three of them just idly follow him up to the bank and when he walked down on the sidewalk with his money for his bale of cotton, one of 'em would jab him in the belly with a pistol from one side and one on the other and he'd look around and there'd be half a dozen of 'em standing around with a tote bag and their thumb hanging on their pistol belt and they'd take his money and dare him to tell somebody about it. They went out in the woods and find some old boy making whiskey up there somewhere and they'd tell him, "We brought you a sack of hops and a sack of whatever else it took to make several gallons of whiskey, and we'll be back here two weeks from tonight and we want you to have us ten gallons of whiskey.

Well, if you're watchin' what you're doing when you're working as a peace officer, there's something about being quick enough to grasp the truth about something when it comes in front of you. Things like that happened all along, things you can see every time you turn around. When I lived over there in East Texas, I had pretty much of a reputation for gaining confessions from thugs of all kinds, from murderers, arsonists, rapists, and what have you. I was always watching, trying to figure out who might make a good informer. Made friends with people, gained their trust. One guy I picked washed cars in the back of one of the car garages there. I had him wash my car every once in awhile. I fiddled around with him for a month or two, jerking my pistol out, teasing, and he would say, "Oh My God, Ranger Bishop, quit scaring me like that!" One day I decided to ask him about a man who I knew had killed an old fellow for not making whiskey for him. He said, "Yes, I sure do know him, but if he ever knew I talked to you, my life wouldn't be worth five cents." I said, "Well, he won't ever know it from me. Anything you tell me will be absolutely confidential and I want you to help me catch him." Two or three weeks later he came to me and said, "Mr. Bishop, the man you want lives in such and such deserted old house down in the south part of the county.

My folks still lived in Del Rio, and I didn't have my own car. So I borrowed Dan Hines' little new Chevrolet, didn't make no noise a'tall on that old sandy road, and drove right up in front of that house. Dan didn't go with me, I don't know why, he was my partner there at the time. All the others had come and gone. The house was an old log place, the chinkin' had fallen out between the logs, but it still had an old home-made board floor and I could hear the man runnin' inside. I had that Thompson machine gun with me, and a shot gun and a rifle or two. This little ole house had been there for years, and the brush all around it had closed in where it wasn't more than thirty feet from the back door to the timber that you couldn't stick a butcher knife in. The car hadn't even stopped rolling when I realized my target was about to get away. I threw the car door open and jumped out and went around the house as fast as I could run. I was a lot younger then than I am now, and could run pretty fast. I went around there and just as I rounded the last corner there he was, just about to get into the brush. I hollered at him and called him by name. He had an old Tom rifle of some kind, an old 38, 56, 45, 70 or something like that, an old timer with a brass plate right under where the lever hung on. By golly when I come around there and hollered at him, he just whirled and fired, I mean just that quick. He just turned and brought that old gun up and I was lookin' right in the mouth of it. I guarantee you it looked as big as a dinner plate. And he fired just as quick as he come up with it. And like I said, I was running just as fast as I could, and I thought he was going to kill me. I don't ever remember when I pulled my gun at all, but I know I didn't pull it until I saw him and saw he was gonna shoot me and I just threw myself out of the way as I was a runnin'....I just threw myself to one side and I had pulled my pistol in time for his

Dan Hines (left) and Leo Bishop (right).

bullet to go in my scabbard. I always carried my billfold in my right hip pocket, and it went in my pistol scabbard right in the mouth of it and out the back side of it and through my billfold and cut the $180...I'd just cashed a pay check...right half in two and right through the cheek of my behind and out the seat of my britches. Pretty big jar, too, big old lead bullet big as the end of my finger. Kinda turned me over in the air as I was a-fallin'. But anyway, I shot at him. And I didn't shoot at him to shoot his trigger finger off, I shot at him to kill him. But he had that gun up just right so that my bullet shot two of his fingers off, trigger finger off at the second knuckle and shot this other one off, just one knuckle off of it, I believe. My old .45 slug just knocked his old gun right out of his hand, of course it jarred him pretty bad, too. And he just throwed up his hands when he dropped that gun, went to beggin' me not to kill him. I was laying' there on my side just ready to shoot him again and I don't know why I didn't. He needed killin'...I oughta just saved the state the expense of tryin' him...and I had a perfect right to kill him because he'd just shot at me. But, I didn't. I disarmed him accidentally with the first shot, and he was just standin' there pleading with me not to shoot him and I didn't have the gall to go ahead and shoot him down in cold blood, I wouldn't do...I never did do it.

I got up, struggled around a little bit and by gosh I could stand up, my behind felt like it was all shot off, but I could feel something runnin' down my britches leg, I didn't know if it was red or yellow, but I walked on over there and picked up his gun. I drove him around to the front of the house where the car had stopped, got the key out of the switch and raised the turtle back, and searched him, made him bend over under that turtle back, searched him good and he didn't have no other arms...saw he had 2, 3, or 4 more cartridges in his pocket, none of them the same caliber. That old gun he had had two or three different calibers in it, but the one he fired at me damn sure fired. I put my handcuffs on him and put him in that turtle back and locked him down in it...it was just a little coupe...a Chevrolet coupe. I locked him up in there and decided I'd better see how bad I was shot. So I got my britches down, found out that was blood running down my legs and my boot was about full by that time with blood. I was bleeding pretty good...had two holes in me back there...went in and went out again, just made a trench. Anyway, I decided I wasn't hurt very bad, got myself pulled all back up and got my six-shooter finally located off that sore spot, got in and cranked up, drove on back to San Augustine...18 or 20 miles.

I drove up to the old jail yard, it was right on the courthouse square. I drove in there in front of the jail and got out. I was pretty stiff by that time and couldn't hardly walk...I was in front of the jail and didn't want any of them folks to know I'd come mite near getting killed. Some of them might think they could get it done. So I didn't tell anybody about it or anything and decided not to let anybody see just how bad crippled I was. I unlocked that thing and let my prisoner out of the back and led him right on into the jail and took my handcuffs off of him, locked him up in a cell, and said, "If you decide you want to break jail, you just break out, 'cause I'm gonna kill you when you hit the ground."

He was a mean son-of-a-gun, weighed about 175-180 pounds, about 5 feet 8 or 9 inches tall, about 35 years old. Anyway, the second morning after I put him in jail, before I got down town good, somebody come and told me...they got a jail break. So I rushed down to the jail to see what in the world had happened and there wasn't any break to it, the doors was all standin' wide open, and my prisoner had escaped. Next time I caught him was in Oklahoma City. I brought him back then, they tried him and give him fifty years in the pen. While he was there, someone killed him with an ice pick. He had been one of that bunch of henchmen of this band of Special Rangers that Ma Ferguson had over there in San Augustine, that was robbin' and killin'… they done everything you can think of. I could set here and just remember all night long different crimes that was committed right there in that town by that bunch of thugs.

Interviewer: What were they doing?

BISHOP: Everything. They even robbed widow women. They even went out there in the country and an old widow woman lived there and had a couple big ole fat hogs in a pen was just fer winters' meat, and damn if they didn't go out there and kill all them hogs and drug 'em out and her beggin' 'em not to and carried 'em off and ate themselves and left her without anything. They'd do anything for two bits up to whatever they could git for it. They whupped this Federal man over there and beat him nearly to death at one of their county fairs. This bunch of thugs did. The Government had sent this man in there… there was some counterfeiting going on. These guys were behind that, too. You can't name any crime that I can't tell you somebody had committed while I was over there.

I done two hitches in San Augustine. The first time I went there and stayed three months, 90 days, through a term of court…and sent nineteen of 'em to the penitentiary and electric chair the first term of court, and the first one they had had there in years. I told the commissioners, "The governor sent me over here to clean things up, and I'm gonna do it." They was pretty scared to death of me anyway. I'd made everybody over there think I was the meanest man in town.

When I left there, they pulled me out of there and brought me back to Del Rio and eventually on down to South Texas. Anyway, I stayed over there a second time. I was gone from San Augustine just exactly a year. Some of the people I sent to the penitentiary the first time just got a year's sentence. And when that year began to play out, the better class of people, business people who were still in the town over there, some of them kin to these damn outlaws that I'd sent to the penitentiary...there were just thirty of them got in a bunch and come all the way to Austin and asked Governor Allred...told him the circumstances. They told him a bunch of men had been sent to the pen who had killed people and shot 'em in bed at night and they never did know what had happened, done everything else to 'em and said, "We know the day they come back our lives ain't worth five cents because we sat on the juries that sent 'em up. Old Colonel Carmichael told 'em, we'll send you a good Ranger over there. They said, "No, we don't want nobody but Leo Bishop, we won't have nobody but Leo Bishop." Well, I was down at Hebbronville, in South Texas, helping old Captain Dale McMurray run them damn outlaws around down there in them prickly pear, about to get killed myself. So, that day here come orders to take up my station in San Augustine, certain day at 9:00 o'clock. I said, "I served my hitch over there, and I don't want to go back. Captain, if you can't do somethin' about this, why I'll quit before I'll go over there." "Well," he said, "Let's go to Austin."

We got in his car and rushed up there and talked to old Colonel Carmichael. I said, "I want to talk to Governor Allred. I ain't going back over there. I mean it. I want to talk to Governor Allred." Colonel Carmichael, a great big man, weighed over 300 pounds, said, "Well, the governor's busy, but I'll be glad to see if there is anything I can do for you." So he sent word in there, and the governor told him, "Yes, he would talk to me." Well, I just dashed right on around to his office and when I walked in he met me at the door and shook hands with me and slapped me on the back and said, "Boy, it's sure good to see you. Just keep up the good work!" And he shoved me back out the door and shut the door. He didn't even give me the chance to tell him what I'd come over there to say. Well, I was terribly disgusted and disheartened and went on back in there to Colonel Carmichael. He said, "The reason we're sending you back over there is that there was thirty of them people come over here in a bunch and demanded that they wouldn't have anybody but you. Just go on back to Hebbronville and get your gear, and go on over there."

So, by then I needed a job pretty bad. By that time I had three queens and a pair of jacks plus my wife that I was tryin' to make a livin' for. I was kinda anxious to get away from down there, too...I was gonna have to kill two or three of them outlaws if I stayed there, or get killed. They'd already threatened me. When I got down there I hired a little ole truck, didn't have nothin' but a saddle and a trunkful of clothes. They took it over to San Augustine. Me and my wife and kids got in a little old Ford I had and drove to San Augustine. When we got in there that night them people had rented us a house, this three or four room house, already rented from somebody, and they had every room full of furniture, bedroom suite and everything you can think of that was good to eat...one end of the kitchen was stacked to the ceiling with hams, sacks of flour, buckets of coffee and cans of peaches, just a truckload of it. There were clean linens, the table was set with new silverware, nothing fine but just good common sense stuff.

Interviewer: You did have a lot of good friends over there who appreciated you?

BISHOP: Well, Christmas time had come to me and it wasn't even Christmas. I just couldn't believe it. My wife just stood there speechless. The kids the same way. Them people, about forty of them, had met us and escorted us down to our new home, and they was standing around there elbowin' each other...laughin'...at the look we had on our faces, I reckon. We went to bed, by George just give out, just wore out, my wife was sick, too. We stayed over there three years that time. I'll guarantee you everything stayed the same the whole three years we were there. Them people would just come up to my house and get the baby and take her downtown, and they'd bring her back completely dressed...from the hide out...new shoes, new dress, new panties, new everything. But, every two or three days somebody else would come get her down there...you never saw nothin' like it. They bought me suits of clothes, overcoats and shirts and boots and hats. We would wake up in the morning and there'd be sweet potatoes fresh dug out of somebody's patch settin' on my back porch and I never would know who done it. And over in another big box there'd be a fresh butchered hog...you know, one of them old long-nosed razor backed, cleaned, ready to eat. Things like that happened to us all the time we lived there...three years.

Interviewer: Were you shot at many times? You said you carried two six guns and a rifle.

BISHOP: No, that's the reason I wasn't shot at, because I carried the battle to them. I didn't wait for them to come huntin' me or give them a chance to hide behind a corner or something and shoot me. I was a'huntin' them all the time. Just as fast as I could find one I'd tell him he better be prepared all the time, cause I was watchin'. When I found out who they were, I just run a bluff on them, and that's the only reason I lived through it. I know Homer Garrison would tell you the same thing today if he was living. Once, though, I did get four shots through the leg. I was in the hospital...carried my britches and everything in there....one small hole gimme a lot of trouble before I could even walk on it. Christmas time came along while I was back home in bed, and a friendly negro came up to my door, handed my wife a little old envelope that said, "Christmas Present" and he told the name of the man who sent it.

She said, "He's up there in bed in the front room, please come on in and give it to him."

Well, the package had a hundred and some odd dollars in there, and a list of all the people who had paid a dollar to ten or fifteen or twenty dollars...you know, just a Christmas present, something I really needed bad at the time. God knows how bad I needed it, 'cause I had such a big family and doctor bills and everything. They did things like that for me and tried their best. When I left San Augustine at the end of three years, the last time, they begged me to quit the Ranger Service and they'd hire me and I wouldn't have no bosses. "Just run the county like you've been doing," they said. They wanted me to stay.

Interviewer: Do you mind if I back-track just a bit? I'd like to get some information about a time that is so important to history. Because there's not much evidence that can be found during the 1930s and 1940s about anybody. I knew your name and everything else, and that you were here. The records, for example...the Department of Public Safety, you know Chief Pharies, after Carmichael died, and everything else...the attorney took the records with him. And they don't start 'til 1937 to the present. The attorney just picked up the records and took them with him. So there's no reports, and most of the people didn't keep their reports, just kept a scrapbook.

BISHOP: Back until the Department of Public Safety was organized, we weren't required to keep our reports at all.

Interviewer: I'm just wondering, do you know what the struggle was after '35 to '37, in there? The commission was composed, you know, the three-man Public Safety Commission. The Sheriffs Association was trying to demand that they have a sheriff on it. Tell us about Ma Ferguson, about being fired, and that they were trying to keep you on.

BISHOP: Well, old man John Martin, manager of the Indio Ranch, had supported Ma Ferguson in her race for Governor and he thought he had enough pull with her because of that, and that she'd keep the Texas Rangers on the Indio Ranch for the same kind of protection that we'd been giving them there for about ten months. And he asked us to go to Austin. And he met us in Austin and he and Arch Miller the Sergeant of the Company and Red Humphreys and he requested Ma Ferguson to keep us in the Ranger Service. And she "kow-towed" with him for two or three days down there and caused us to have to pay a good-sized hotel bill, and then we end up gettin' letters from her that our services had terminated the day she was inaugurated as Governor.

So we came on back home and went to lookin' for honest jobs. The first one I got was I broke five wild horses for a man for $25.00, five dollars a head. And then the next job I got was working for Cotton Whitehead, one of the biggest ranchmen in this area for $25.00 a month, runnin' a pack of hounds and settin' traps to keep the coyotes from killin' a string of sheep that he had moved down about half way between Del Rio and Eagle Pass. I worked for him thirty days and my wife came down there one night way in the night with a telegram from Lone Wolf Gonzaullas over at Longview, Texas, tellin' me that If I could get over there, wear both six-shooters and carry my sawed-off shotgun and my raincoat, he'd give me a job, $5.00 a night, straight time.

So I went into Del Rio with my wife that night, and saw Cotton Whitehead next morning to get my $25.00. I had worked for him just exactly a month and explained the situation to him and showed him the telegram and told him I had to go because this job would help take care of my family, and he gave me my check for my wages and I took it to the bank and they turned it down. Wouldn't give me a nickel on it. And he was one of the biggest operators in this country...ranchman with approximately 100 sections of ranchland stocked at that time. But, that's how tough the depression days were.

Interviewer: That's hard to believe, isn't it?

BISHOP: I borrowed $20.00 from a friend of mine, old man E.F. Measles, the manager of the Eagle Pass Lumber Company and went to East Texas and went to work for Gonzaullas and the Atlas Pipeline Company at a station in Kilgore, Texas. After I'd been there 4, 5, or 6 days, why here comes another old river rat Ranger from down in Crystal

City, W.E. Riggs, who passed away about a month ago, and I was one of his pallbearers. Anyway, he came over there and they put him on that same station with me. He and I worked from 7 o'clock in the evening to 7 o'clock the next morning, seven days a week.

Interviewer: Gonzaullas wasn't a Ranger at this time, was he? He was a Special Ranger too?

BISHOP: Yeah, he'd been fired the same time I was...

Interviewer: How did the Rangers feel about Gonzaullas, would you mind telling me?

BISHOP: Oh, nearly all of 'em liked him all right. But they all thought like I did, that he was just a big bunch of bull, you know, because he put out that kind of stuff all the time about what a tough guy I was, and the best shot in the Ranger Service, and built me up a terrible reputation to where I was scared I was gonna get killed before I ever got to the job. After Riggs and I drew a paycheck we both got our families moved over there. My wife drove from Del Rio with four little kids down through Houston and up to Kilgore.

Interviewer: Why did Gonzaullas want you so bad?

BISHOP: Well, I suppose because of my reputation as best rifle shot in the Ranger Service and that kind of stuff. He put out that kind of baloney after he got me over there. He told everybody around the oil fields what a tough son-of-a-gun I was, and what a good shot I was. It scared 'em up so bad that there wasn't any more damage done on any of the property owned by the Atlas Pipeline Company after he put out this stuff and hired a bunch of us river Rangers over there. ...Anyway, Gonzaullas put me to work the next morning at Kilgore, Texas, biggest

pump station they had. I stayed there four months with that outfit and came back to Del Rio, Texas.

Interviewer: You were a private in the Rangers?

BISHOP: No, I wasn't in the Rangers at the time. I just had a Special Commission under Ma Ferguson then, it was under her administration. She had issued a Special Ranger Commission so that we'd have authority to wear arms. I went to work for the Federal Intermediate Credit Bank in Houston, Texas after I came back down here and was working for them still...inspecting ranches and livestock all over this ranch country when Jimmy Allred ran for Governor and was elected. A friend of mine, Stanford Payne, wanted me back in the Ranger Service, so he talked to Jimmy Allred, the Governor, about it and I was the first man appointed in the Ranger Service the next day after Mr. Allred was inaugurated as Governor. He appointed two other men, one of them a Captain Fred L. McDaniels who had been sheriff four years in Archer County, and Sid Kelso, and me, the only private in the company.

Interviewer: You said you finally had five kids, didn't you? How did you phrase that awhile ago?

BISHOP: "Three queens and a pair of jacks." This other one came on later, after I had gotten in the Ranger Service again. When Governor James V. Allred was elected Governor I was the first man he appointed back into the Ranger Service. I went to San Augustine.

Interviewer: Before you go back to San Augustine...could you mention anything that you learned from experience on the border to stay alive or that you remember as technique or anything other that you'd learned when you've been on your ranch? Tell me, did the old Rangers that you know, that they tried to break you in with, did they teach you anything special? I know you were telling me about Levi Duncan... did you teach him anything specifically? Other than just showing him around?

BISHOP: I told him my experiences. When he was appointed to the Ranger Service and sent to me at Del Rio, I took him down on the Indio Ranch where I'd gotten some experience with them Mexicans down there, stealing them cattle from across the border all the time, and left him down there a'foot, horseback for a month or two, and I'd go by to see him and ask him how he'd been getting along and I was trying him out because at the time when he came down there I was under the impression that Levi hadn't ever been anything but a professional gambler. He was a card shark, and dice...he could really take your money away from you, if you weren't as sharp as he was. He wasn't really the kind of man I would have thought that Governor Allred would have put in the Ranger Service as a fightin' man because he didn't have any fight in him. He'd rather talk you out of it or play you poker for it or something like that. He put up a good front and he was a good fellow, though.   All Levi knew was race horses and playin' poker and shootin' dice. He could sure tell you about that and show you. I sat in on a few poker games with him and saw how he could stack the deck and give you four aces and give the man next to you a full house and right on around the table...and whoever he wanted to win the pot, he gave that man the best hand. He tried to show me, but I couldn't see it. But anyway, I thought lots of him. Levi. He was still in the Rangers after I quit. They told him one time when he was stationed here at Del Rio to come over to Rock Springs to stop the gambling up there. There'd been two or three preachers and some church ladies had written into headquarters asking them to send somebody to this little town because there were some poker games going on and the like. So they sent the message to Levi to go up there and stop the gambling. He went up there and got in the poker game and won all their money and that stopped the gambling. But anyway, he's gone now.

Interviewer: Yeah, we saw him. We interviewed him just briefly about two months before he died.

BISHOP: Once Levi was with me, I believe we were going from Eagle Pass through a cut-off road to Uvalde. I was driving. At the time I was wearing two six-shooters. The people over in East Texas…San Augustine…had made me a present of a pair of .45 single action pistols because I had gotten the situation under control over there. It was late in the afternoon and the sun was to our back, and I saw a big old rattlesnake four or five feet long crossing the road ahead of us. He was going far enough ahead of us that by the time we got there, going 35 or 40 miles an hour on that country road, he had already gotten off in the ditch. As we went by I pulled my left hand pistol and shot out the window and shot the rattlesnake's head off. And I said, "I made a good shot, Levi." He looked back through the window and said, "Stop, stop…I've got to see that!" So I put on my brakes and backed the old Chevrolet up there and this old snake was just whippin' around there, you know, with his head gone. Accidents will happen, you know.

Interviewer: Do you remember what year, approximately, (you were accidentally shot)?

BISHOP: That was about in '34, I guess, somewhere along in there. Jimmy Allred was governor, and I was patrolling that ship channel in Houston where Captains...

Interviewer: Oh, that was that Houston strike?

BISHOP: Maritime Strike.

Interviewer: That was in 1935 or '36, I believe.

BISHOP: And I happened to be sent off with Captain Myer, who had been in the Department School up at Austin. He had been trainin' people how to use firearms. He was a firearms expert. He was teachin' the people up there in the Department School how to use firearms. He was driving a patrol car and he had a .22 rifle right between us and he saw a hawk flyin' around there up in the sky. He just put on his brakes and lookin' out at that hawk and threw the door of that old Ford open and just reached back and got this little old gun by the stock and this old Ford was one of them floorboard kind of transmissions, you know, and the gun barrel was sticking between that emergency brake and that transmission lever and without lookin' back even as he stepped out he reached back and got it and pulled it around there and it went off and shot me right through my thigh there. Well, it went in and hit the bone and splattered. Anyway, he had to take me into the hospital and get all that lead cut out of my leg. About two weeks after that in his home there in Houston he was cleaning his pistol in his living room, he let his gun go off and shot the rocker off a chair his wife was sittin' in.

Interviewer: And this was a gun expert, huh?

BISHOP: Yeah, he was the one they had training people in the use of firearms up there in the DPS school.

Interviewer: What happened to him?

BISHOP: Oh, I don't know. I don't think they fired him, or anything like that. He was a Captain of the Highway Patrol.

Interviewer: They say you can look at a man….or a man has a certain look or a certain gaze come into his eyes…they say they can tell you when a man's gonna kill you.

BISHOP: Yeah, I think that's right. I faced a man down in East Texas with a shot gun one time when a dipping situation over there, the State Livestock Sanitary Commission was dipping all their livestock trying to kill these fever ticks out of the last ten counties there in East Texas. Old man Bob Martin, who had a seat on the last Livestock Sanitary Commission of Texas, got the Adjutant General old Colonel H.H. Carmichael to designate me as an official pistol packer on that work over there. One day I had to go with 2, 3, or 4 other men, their inspectors for this Livestock Sanitary Commission, and take a shotgun away from an old man. He had beat up one of their inspectors and turned all the cattle out at the dipping vats and run 'em off in the woods and dared 'em to come back and get his I believe fourteen head, cost him $28.00 at $2.00 a head for fourteen head. Anyway, when we went over there to get him, why he stepped out on his front porch with an automatic 12-gauge shotgun and levelled it right down on us. We 'wuz still settin' in the car and he went to callin' us every mean word he could think of and gonna kill the first man who hit the ground and since I was the fightin' man for the outfit, why it looked like it was just up to me to do somethin' about it. I crawled out of the car with him threatenin' to kill me when I hit the ground and he didn't. Of course I was a watchin' him, he was a great big old stout fellow. I walked out… of course he had the drop on me, lookin' right down the barrel of that 12-gauge automatic shotgun at me. Well, we went out there to git him, we didn't go out there to be runoff. We went out there because he had violated the law and beat up this Inspector. That was the job to go and bring him to justice. When I got out of the car he didn't shoot me, so I decided he didn't mean all he was saying to us. I went over to the yard gate. He had a big yard, a big old house way up on stilts. His old lady was standing there right by him holding the screen door open for him up on this big high porch. I walked in the yard gate, still he was cussin' me all the time, threatenin' to shoot me every step but he still didn't do it. I walked right up on the porch with stairs going up to it. He was holdin' that shotgun on me all the way, daring me to come another step and cussin' with every breath, all the profanity you ever heard he was usin' it. And when I got right up to the foot of these steps and was fixin' to walk right on up there with him, he just stepped back inside that door and laid that shotgun up against that door-jamb and said, "You come in my house, I'm gonna kill you." I, of course, was lookin' him right in the eye all the time and I saw the gleam in his eye then…he did intend to kill me and he would have shot me off that porch if I'd of started up in his house.

Interviewer: You didn't see it before then?

BISHOP: No, I knew when he stood back there, and the way he said it, he was fixin' to kill me. I still hadn't had a chance to pull my gun at all because he had me covered all the time. Anyway, I stood right there and faced him and talked to him about it and everything and the trouble he was in…a shame to do his wife that away and I don't know what all, a lot of stuff until I talked him away from that door. He backed up inside the room where I couldn't see him. When he did that, I ran around the house and came in the back door and his wife had outrun me to the back screen door and just latched the screen as I got there. The screen door was onto a screened porch.

I said, "Lady, you better unlatch your door, 'cause I'm a'comin' through. No use in you havin' to buy a screen door as well as bury your husband. I'm comin' in after him." She just stood there and looked at me for a minute and just reached over and unlocked it. I jumped in the house and of course, I had one of my pistols in my hand and I was ready to do battle with him. When I stepped in on this porch she said, "Oh My God, Oscar, he's in the house and he's got his gun in his hand." When she said that…I could see down this porch and right on out through the front, there was a hallway like through there and I heard that old shotgun hit the floor and old Oscar ran out where I could see him with his hands up. Oh, he was a wild-eyed feller then 'cause he was scared. I guess when she told him I was in the house and had my gun out…so, I just walked right on down there to him and punched him around pretty lively with that six-shooter and come on out on that front porch and all them other guys were still sittin' in the car out there, tongue-tied. I took all the rest of the box of shotgun shells he had…he had a jumper pocket in them blue-bib overalls, had every pocket full of buckshot shells. Took him out there and turned him over to them, then I went back in there…he'd throwed this old shotgun over behind an old-time trunk. We took him on into Lufkin and fined him $28.00 for what he did that morning…he had fourteen head of livestock at $2.00 a head…with what the law provided to charge him, pickin' 'em up and dippin' em, by law, which we did when we got the money. I hauled him back out there that afternoon, my wife was with me…she went over to Lufkin with me that morning from San Augustine, where I was stationed, 55 miles over there. *(note: this mileage would be reasonably correct…Highway 103 was not yet constructed… a trip to Lufkin would require going through Nacogdoches.)*

My wife stood there, and pleaded with me, to tell Hardy Purvis the whole story about what happened. Hardy Purvis, at that time, was my captain. Best one I ever had.

After I got this all straightened out, got that old man's cattle all rounded up, and hauled him back out to his farm, eight miles, and put him out where his road turned off about half a mile off the pavement. It was late in the afternoon. He got out of the car, and he just stood there by me, rubbing his feet around in the sand and lookin' down at the ground…I knew he wanted to say something. I said, "What'cha got on your mind, Oscar?" He said, "Well, young feller, I want to tell you something. I've killed three men in my life and I intended to kill you this morning and I just don't know now why I didn't." I hoorawed him a little and said, "Aw, you didn't have the guts enough." Then I said, "We're going to be back over here in fourteen days to dip your cattle again and I don't want no trouble out of you, 'cause if there's any shootin' done from now on I'm gonna do it." Handed him a pretty good threat, but it didn't do no good. Not long after that they moved me plum out of that country, in fact back to Del Rio, and the old man whipped another Inspector with an axe-handle, nearly beat him to death at one of the dippings. Eventually sold all of his livestock he had, to keep them from dipping them under the law.

No one had told me that the old man had killed three men... I mighta been a lot more careful. But anyway, I talked him out of it at the time.

Interviewer: Is this kind of a technique you've learned?

BISHOP: I just used whatever came into my mind, to try and get by, without having to kill a man...just ingenuity. I think, they talk about men being born to a particular job sometimes. I think a real good peace officer is born with that in him. You can't train it in him. I've had various experiences in my lifetime as a peace officer and I spent about twenty or twenty-five years at it, deputy sheriff and jobs beside the Ranger Service, and I have run into guys that had a pistol-packing job that they were "a round peg in a square hole"...there's no way in the world that they could do anything right. They did everything wrong. Some of them got killed over it, and a lot of them never did get the job done because they didn't know what to do under the circumstances.

Interviewer: You talked earlier about Gonzaullas...you also talked about Sterling...can you discuss W.W. Sterling?

BISHOP: Well, he was a fine fellow, W.W. Sterling was, and was one of the great Texas Rangers and did some fine work, but he was also a guy that wore flashy clothes and flashy boots and the biggest hat that Stetson could make and beautiful pistols, people gave 'em to him for work that he had done in the oil fields and places like that. But he wore 'em sticking in his boot part of the time, you know. He wasn't the only guy I knew like that. We had a Captain of the Ranger Service one time, named Red Hawkins. I've seen him walk down the streets of Del Rio with a big pearl-handled six-shooter stuck in each boot. Just show-off, you know, that's all it amounted to. He was a good officer, too, but, some officers, I guess that's what you call goin' to their head a little bit, when they put a six shooter on 'em they couldn't help but show off a little bit. It didn't mean they wasn't a good officer, most of the time, but they just had a little bit of showmanship in their makeup. You couldn't blame 'em for it, but there was a lot of guys that wasn't like that, that was just as good officers, or maybe better than they were, but they didn't show off their equipment and their authority and all that kind of stuff. They didn't use it for showmanship. They carried their pistol under their coat most of the time, and if they went into a town, maybe they didn't want everybody there to know that they were a two-gun pistol packer and that they was there to take whoever they was sent there to take and whatever circumstances might arise. They were just a different kind of peace officers.

Interviewer: Do you think Captain Hickman was the same type as that?

BISHOP: No, not near as much. He liked to go to rodeos. He liked to ride and lead the parade, Texas Ranger and everything, but he didn't dress as flashy as Gonzaullas and Sterling did. He didn't show off his sidearms and all that kind of stuff as much as they did. Although he was a showman to some extent. And personally, I never did like Tom Hickman near as well as I liked Gonzaullas or Bill Sterling either one. He....I don't hardly know how to express it, but he never did impress me as being a man that would come up on the firing line when it was necessary and stand there 'till the last bullet went by.

Interviewer: Do you know of anything else that would make you aware when you were trying to apprehend somebody, or when you would look at somebody, other than their eyes, that would be an indication of danger? Or what to do?

BISHOP: Well, a lot of it would depend on a man's reputation, which I nearly always would know before I was able to overtake him and apprehend him. What kind of a guy he would be, whether he was trigger happy or dangerous or not. Personally I never did want to die with my boots on from being shot by some outlaw that I was trying to apprehend, and I always tried to keep the advantage from the time I got there until I had him locked up. Several good friends I've had killed that-away just from pure negligence. When they'd apprehend somebody they didn't search him good and he'd come out with a gun and kill 'em on the way to jail. I never did want that to happen to me, and I always was extremely watchful and extremely careful in trying to prevent that happening.

Interviewer: That's what you mean by advantage? You were always watching him all the time?

BISHOP: Absolutely. From the time I got there until I had the complete advantage of him...after completely searching him, putting handcuffs on him, taking him to jail, well, I didn't give him a chance to do anything to me. Or make any effort, otherwise I'd have to kill him if he had.

Interviewer: Would you use your voice at times?

BISHOP: Absolutely. I'd always tell a man who I was, as a rule, and demand that he get his hands up immediately, or maybe if I thought it was necessary, I'd cover him with my pistol before he had a chance to know who I was. I'd just jerk my gun out. I'd never get right up against a man if I thought he was going to cause trouble, 'cause he'd have a chance to take my gun away from me. I always kept him at a distance...say ten feet away, and demand that he put his hands up on a wall until I'd searched him or something like that. If I thought he was a dangerous character I just took all the advantage. I didn't give him any at all until I had him under complete control, thereby giving him no chance...where I didn't have to kill him.

Well, I just didn't want anybody's blood on my hands if I could keep it from happenin' ...And that's the best way for a good officer to keep it from happenin' ...keep complete advantage all the time of anybody you meet...that's to handle 'em.

I never drew on a man with the intention of killing him...I figured I drew on 'em to get the drop on 'em to keep him from making an effort to kill me. And tellin' him about it in a loud tone of voice at the time so that it would paralyze any action that he might want to take.

Thereby I took him before he had time to get his mind a'workin' ...had my cuffs on him, and his gun offa him and had him helpless at my mercy just by my action, quick, fast, and deliberate, like you say, on a number of occasions. I've called a man an ugly name to paralyze his thoughts for a minute, you know. That's the effect it has on somebody. It takes a lot of hide out of a man if you just hand him something like that all unexpected like, then you'd follow right on up with it. You take charge of him before he realizes what's happened because you did kinda paralyze his thoughts for a moment.

The Circa 1900 Fussell Cotton Gin Company, intersection of the Ayish Bayou and El Camino Real de los Tejas National Historic Trail.

Workers at the Fussell Cotton Gin witnessed the ambush and killing of a prominent citizen during the 1930s crime wave in San Augustine.

Leo Bishop and Ruby Nation married in 1921. With a bit of financial assistance from his dad Buck Bishop, Leo purchased a small ranch near Carta Valley, Texas. The couple settled down, raising cattle and starting their family. A few years later Leo sold this property and bought another ranch in nearby Terrell County in the Pecos River region. The Great Depression of 1929 did not treat the Leo Bishop family kindly.

In 1935 governor James Allred appointed L.J. Wardlow chairman of the Livestock Sanitary Commission in an effort to eradicate Texas of its tick infestation. This is the law that created the requirement that all cattle be dipped, and one which Ranger Leo Bishop enforced repeatedly, and with great success, throughout the Deep East Texas area.

The following excerpts from the transcribed Dictabelt interview describe events that actually prove that <u>truth</u> finally wins out...in the grand scheme of life's happenings.

BISHOP: As a result of several incidents having to do with the dipping law, the Chairman of the Livestock Sanitary Commission, old Judge L.J. Wardlow, one time ran for Governor, lived in Fort Worth. He came all the way to San Augustine and he had a good reason to dislike me from what he knew about me because I'd been pretty badly misrepresented to him by a brother of his who had closed me out of the Ranch business before I got in the Ranger Service. And his brother had told Judge Wardlow I was a damn fool and liable to kill some innocent man...I was trigger happy and all that kind of stuff. And so, when he learned from his Inspectors about the success I was having with this dipping law enforcement...in spite of opposition from those who said "they didn't have to dip...wasn't nobody big enough to make 'em dip." Anyway, when the smoke was kinda settled over all this stuff, here comes Judge L.J. Wardlow, gets him a room in a local hotel there in this little town of San Augustine where I lived and called me up and asked me to come down...he wanted to talk to me. I went down there and he asked me to have a seat. I knew he didn't like me and I didn't like him, because his name was Wardlow...I'd never seen him before, but I didn't like his brother a'tall, he robbed me with a pencil point instead of a pistol point.

Interviewer: This was in '29, you mean when you lost everything? He was the one that had done it?

BISHOP: Yeah. His brother, who lived here (Del Rio). He was the head of the State Loan concern, President of the Bank and everything. Anyway, manhandled me pretty good, broke me of about $180,000.

BISHOP: So when Judge Wardlow came down there, I just didn't like him 'cause of his brother and I knew what his brother had told him about me. And I wouldn't even sit down when he invited me to sit down and talk to him back in the room for quite awhile. He finally... he was a pretty tough old codger...he told me, "I want to tell you something. I don't want you feelin' that way towards me, I know why you feel that way and all that, but you've been pretty badly misrepresented to me and I want to tell you about it. I was told that you were a pretty good gun-happy guy when you were appointed in the Ranger Service and that you were liable to kill some innocent man or maybe several of them." And then he said, "I've found out from experience that you've passed up golden opportunities to kill a man in self-defense and you always managed to get by and enforce the law and take him in without killin' him, when you could have done it and never been prosecuted for it."

I appreciated that coming from a man that I knew had reason not to like me, come all the way to East Texas to tell a little old private in the rear-ranks of the Ranger Service, that he thought I was an Okay guy. He told me before I left there, he said, "In spite of all this...the misunderstanding of each other, I hold nothing against you and I appreciate everything you've done for me. And if ever you have to kill somebody, and need a 'damn good lawyer' just call on me, it won't cost you a thing."

Anyway, I appreciated that, you know, coming from a man like that.

Hotel Hampton in San Augustine, Texas where Judge Wardlow and Leo Bishop had their meeting.

Mrs. Mary Bryan's son Hampton Downs was her chosen namesake for the Hampton Hotel. Noted for her hospitality and delicious home-cooked meals, "Miss Mary" welcomed both the traveling public and local townspeople to her spacious facilities at the Hampton Hotel.

Photographer Russell Lee of the Farm Services Administration (FSA) visited San Augustine in 1939 to photograph rural life in America during the Franklin Delano Roosevelt Administration. Lee and his wife Jean enjoyed their stay and amazing food at the Hampton Hotel so much that they remained weeks longer than planned, resulting in thousands of photos taken in the San Augustine vicinity. Lee encouraged his friend and photographer John Vachon, Office of War Information (OWI) to come to San Augustine in 1942 for the large scale informational campaign in the United States relating to World War II. The photographs of both Russell Lee and John Vachon are stored in the Library of Congress and available to the public.

Leo Bishop around 1920, before his marriage to Ruby Nation.

From the Bettye Bishop Robbins Family Collection.

EARLY DAYS
IN CARTA VALLEY, TEXAS

Pictured: A large herd of sheep in the South Texas ranch of Buck and Allene Bishop. Notice the unusual use of timber for fencing. This photo is from the family memorabilia of Bettye Bishop Robbins, Leo's daughter and family historian.

Leo Bishop's GREAT GRANDPARENTS

Wiley Bishop (born 1813 NC) and wife Mary Elizabeth "Eliza" McMullen/Bishop (born 1818)

Leo Bishop's Paternal Grandparents

Joseph Leonard Bishop (born 1844)

Mary Harlow Griffith Bishop (born 1844)

Allene Bishop holding her eldest son,

Leonard Henderson Bishop, AKA Texas Ranger Leo Bishop

Allene Bishop with her son Leo

Family Photos from Bettye Bishop Robbins personal collection

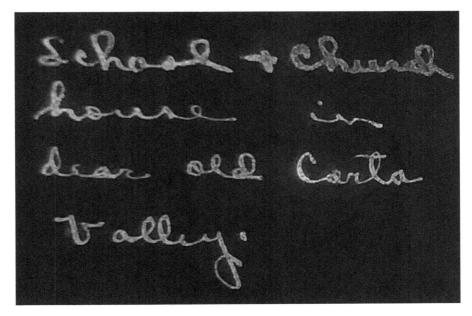

Carta Valley School, Circa 1920's - 1930's

"There's No Place like Home"

Bishop "home place," likely home of the grandparents.

John Cephas "Buck" Bishop (1879-1962) and Laura Allene Henderson Bishop (1880-1978)

Leo Bishop's Parents at their home in Carta Valley.

Buck & Allene Bishop raised their family in this Home

Baby Leo Bishop holding onto the fence with goats nearby.
Someone wrote the caption, "Ain't 'em 'toot" (probably "cute")

Young Leo Bishop about age 12-13 riding the family mule.

Leo Bishop, age 16-17 (the caption read "two dears")

Leo's Dad, "Buck" Bishop, with his dogs.

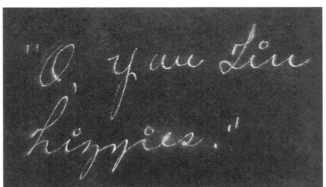

"O, you Tin lizzies."

Above: Leo with his "Tin Lizzie"

Girl in the car with him is likely Ruby Nation.

"Hands up"

"Buck" Bishop and son Leo

Leonard (Leo) Henderson Bishop was the eldest of four sons born to John Cephas Bishop and his wife Laura Allene Bishop. The Texas Ranger Museum website describes his effective law enforcement abilities throughout his 12 year career as a Texas Ranger (1932-1944), including "evidence that led to the conviction of over 100 major criminals."

Leo "Back in the Saddle again!"

Leo Bishop's friends in his younger years in the Carta Valley and Del Rio area. Photo above—Leo's friend Larry.

Photos from a page titled "Friends" in Leo Bishop's personal photo album (with original captions).

Sam.

Ray. H.

Molly.

Edgar.

Ruby Nation's parents Joseph N. Nation (born 1873) and Samantha "MANT" Texana Waldrum Nation (born 1881)

Nation family home in Del Rio, Texas

A young Ruby on horseback in Del Rio, Val Verde County, Tx.

Caption on this photo read "watch out someone is looking."

Leo courting Ruby.

The caption on this photo of Leo and Ruby said "Best Friends."

Ruby (right) with Baylor friend

Caption read "Roses amid thorns"

Ruby Nation and Leo Bishop during their courtship days

Ruby Nation and her Baylor friends at San Felipe Springs in Del Rio, Texas

Fun with friends at the river. Caption read "Scenes at Devils River near home." Leo and Ruby, on right in both photos.

Swimming at Devils River, Texas showing the terrain of the South Texas area.

Leo, Ruby, and friends

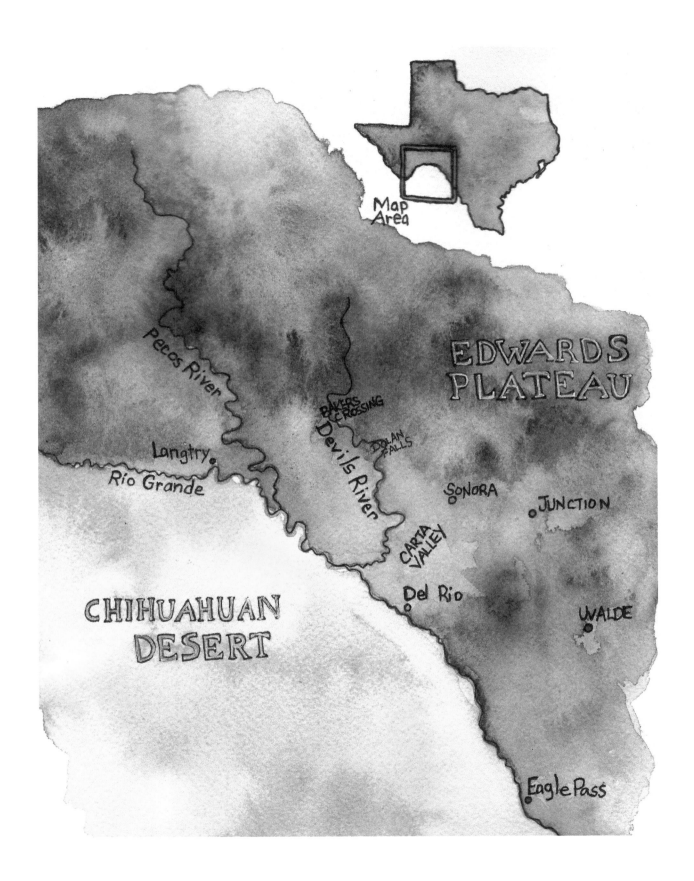

Ruby Nation Bishop, wife of Texas Ranger Leo Bishop, just before their marriage.

Leo Bishop at age 19

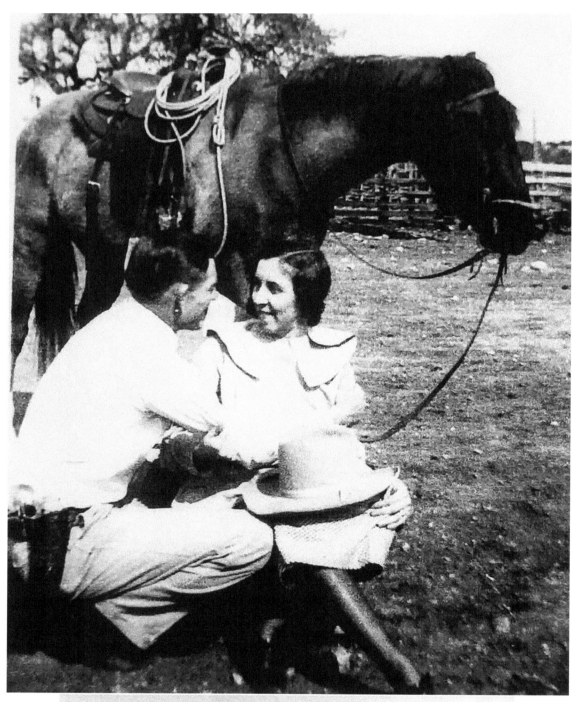

*With all my love for the sweetest
little wife in all the world.
Loving you,
Ted.*

TEXAS RANGER
LEO BISHOP

DURING HIS YEARS IN
SAN AUGUSTINE, TEXAS
1935 AND 1936-1940

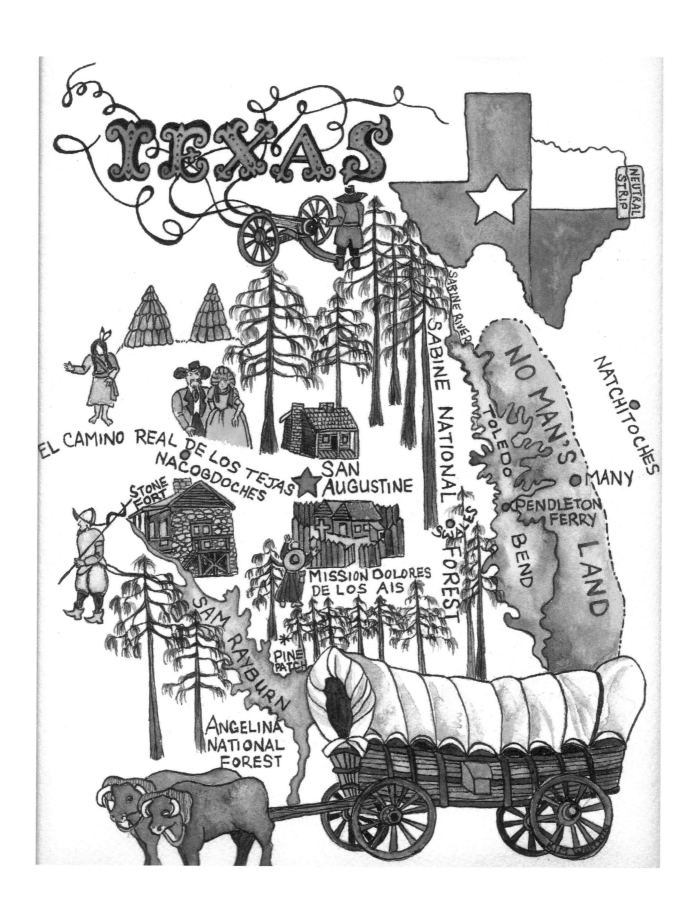

TEXAS

NEUTRAL STRIP

SABINE RIVER

SABINE NATIONAL FOREST

NO MAN'S LAND

NATCHITOCHES

TOLEDO BEND

MANY

PENDLETON FERRY

EL CAMINO REAL DE LOS TEJAS

NACOGDOCHES

STONE FORT

SAN AUGUSTINE

MISSION DOLORES DE LOS AIS

SAM RAYBURN

PINE PATCH

ANGELINA NATIONAL FOREST

San Augustine, Texas courthouse and jail.

Photos by: Russell Lee for FSA Library of Congress collection 1936-1942

CAFÉ TEXAN, later CITY CAFÉ, owned by the Wade Family

Photos by: Russell Lee for FSA, Library of Congress Collection 1936-1942

San Augustine County Clerk Cecil Murphy, 1939

Cecil Murphy served this county for 40 years 1939-1970. His son, San Augustine historian Neal Murphy, was manager of the indexed and digitized county records project in 1997.

Photo by: Russell Lee for FSA, Library of Congress Collection 1936-1942

Publisher/Editor Webster Hays, *San Augustine Tribune*

The San Augustine Tribune has been in the Hays family for more than 100 years. Purchased in 1916 by Publisher/Editor Webster F. Hays, the historic newspaper has continued under the wise leadership of his son, Publisher/Editor Arlan Hays and grandson, Publisher/Editor Stephen Hays.

Photo by: Russell Lee for FSA, Library of Congress Collection 1936-1942

Photos by: Russell Lee for FSA, Library of Congress Collection 1936-1942

"My Daddy Was Texas Ranger Leo Bishop"

An accomplished artist and writer, Bettye Sue Bishop Robbins often contributed articles to the local newspaper in Jasper, Texas. The following story is her personal recollection as a nine-year-old child of events in San Augustine, Texas during the mid-1930s.

Sketch drawn by Bettye Bishop Robbins of her Dad

Our family was on the way to San Augustine from Del Rio on the night of the accident. Daddy had come to move us over to San Augustine to be with him.

Daddy had been sent as a Texas Ranger to San Augustine in 1935 by Governor Allred to clean up the unlawful elements that had literally taken over the town. Within 90 days of his arrival, Daddy had turned in 19 indictments for murder and all the defendants got sentences from 1 to 99 years. Later Daddy was honored at a banquet in Beaumont by Governor Allred. Still later 30 leading citizens of San Augustine made a trip to Austin and requested the Governor to station my Dad to San Augustine permanently.

The townspeople had been terrorized by kidnapping and shooting until they were afraid to be seen talking to the Texas Ranger. He was a handsome man, over six feet tall, dark-haired, steely eyed and square jawed. He carried himself like a man with a purpose. When he stopped walking he backed up against a brick wall. The people of San Augustine began to drop notes at his feet when they passed by. When he'd go to the café for a cup of coffee, he'd find a note between the cup and saucer. This is the way he began to gather evidence to convict the men who were terrorizing the town. The element was so corrupt and violent that Daddy was unwilling to move the family to the town until it was brought under control. There were still bullet holes in the store front plate glass window of the hardware store across the street from the courthouse when we finally moved there a year after my Daddy had begun his cleanup. That night when we were on our way to San Augustine, we were hit by a truck, causing our car to veer out of control into a cornfield. The four of us older children, Carolyn, Gene, Kenneth and me Bettye Sue, were all asleep in the back seat.

We were awakened to find ourselves thrown over into the front seat with Mama and Daddy and the baby, Barbara. We were all unhurt. Someone was notified and they came for us and took us on into San Augustine. When we finally arrived in the middle of the night we were taken to a house and told that our rent had been paid for a whole year. The house was fully furnished and all the furniture was given to us. The kitchen was overflowing with groceries. As a nine year old child, I was attracted to a beautiful blue bowl in the center of the table that was full of fresh fruit. The people of San Augustine were so grateful to their Ranger for having cleaned up the town and making it safe for women and children again, that they couldn't do enough for us. We never paid to see a movie or to have our clothes done at the dry cleaners. These things and more were gladly done for us free. The baby, Barbara, was only about six months old and one day Miss Exa Clark came and got her and she brought her back, Barbara had new shoes, lacy socks, a new lacy dress and a doll or two. She looked pretty as a picture.

My Daddy wrote an article in the newspaper trying to express his feelings about how nice the people were to us. He called it "Christmas Comes More Than Once a Year."

This was all years ago, but I still have in my house one of the night tables from the bedroom suite that was in the house the night we arrived. The beautiful blue bowl that was on the table is still around too, and it isn't even chipped.

My Daddy was Texas Ranger Leo Bishop

CHRISTMAS COMES ONLY ONCE A YEAR

The above is an old saying and in most cases a true one, but Texas Ranger Leo Bishop said Sunday morning that it is different in San Augustine which he most forcibly realized Saturday night when he arrived with his family to find a home completely furnished throughout by his friends here in appreciation of his being stationed in San Augustine permanently by the authorities at Austin to continue the fine program of law enforcement in this county. "This fine spirit of appreciation upon the part of friends here so completely surprised me that I know now that Christmas comes more than once a year in San Augustine," said the popular Ranger as he told a Tribune reporter of the surpise that greeted him upon arrival.

Leo Bishop is one of the best Rangers on the force and withal an expert investigator. He is quiet and friendly and will do no one any violence unless some one "starts" something, in which event he is amply able to take care of himself and enforce the law.

Welcome hangs one every door and window for the Bishops and all are proud to have them as permanent citizens of San Augustine.

The Leo & Ruby Bishop children in San Augustine, Tx.

Left to Right:

Gene holding baby Barbara, Bettye Sue, Carolyn and Kenneth

Citizens Showing Their Appreciation of Bishop

Another instance of appreciation upon the part of the citizenship of San Augustine County for the stationing permanently here of State Ranger Leo Bishop came to light this week when it became known that citizens contributed money for a fine pair of ivory handles for his six... They are embellished with long horn steer heads and lend a wild west effect to these beautiful guns.

A nice suit of clothes was also given to the Ranger this week by the well known firm of A. J. Wood & Bros. with Mr. W. P. Wood making the presentation. Such hearty co-operation and genuine appreciation of this splendid officer shows conclusively that the leading citizens of the city are awakening to law enforcement.

"I want you to really thank these people—I just can't find words to express my feeling," said Ranger Bishop to a Tribune reporter Monday while telling us of his honors above mentioned. It's a hard thing to do. In fact, mere words are inadequate to the situation, but when one can see the gleam of satisfaction and appreciation wreathed all over the face of this good-looking cowboy Ranger it's easy to realize that he means

...ery word of it, and he will just have ...o live his appreciation, and we are assured of that in the beginning. That's no doubt one of the reasons why every one is so nice to Bishop. All realize that there is no camouflage about him—that he is indeed earnest on the job he was sent to complete, that of seeing that law and order prevails in San Augustine County.

LEO BISHOP
Texas Ranger

To the People of San Augustine County

It is utterly impossible for me to express my true feelings and appreciation to you and each of you who so generously contributed to the surprise of my life in the home furnishings and groceries found in my new home upon arrival Saturday night. I knew when assigned to duty in San Augustine that I was coming among fine people, but this kindness upon your part binds me even closer to you and all that I can say is: Thanks a lot and that I hope to be able to repay the favor in duty well done thru the proper enforcement of law and order in San Augustine County for the full protection of all worthy citizens. Respectfully,

LEO BISHOP,
Texas Ranger.

(Adv.)

RANGER TRANSFERRED

Leo Bishop who has been here for the past year, serving as a Ranger under Capt. Will McMurray, _____ with his family for San Augustine Saturday, where they will make their home.

He was very popular in the service, having been stationed in San Augustine previously. That community asked for his return.

Texas Ranger Leo Bishop returned to San Augustine for three years at the request of the San Augustine County citizens. The article above is from one of the South Texas newspapers, among the family papers of Bettye Bishop Robbins, Bishop Family Historian.

(Missing word in the article is "left" with his family for San Augustine.)

DEPARTMENT OF PUBLIC SAFETY

RANGER _____ **Division**

IN THE NAME AND BY THE AUTHORITY OF
The State of Texas

To All to Whom These Presents May Come—GREETINGS:

In the name and by the authority of the State of Texas and under and by virtue of the authority reposed in us by the laws of the State of Texas:

BE IT KNOWN, that the Public Safety Commission, and the Director of the Department of Public Safety of the State of Texas, reposing special trust and full confidence in

the integrity and ability of __LEO BISHOP__

of the city of __Del Rio, Val Verde__ _____County Texas, do by virtue

of the authority vested in us by law, constitute and appoint him a __Texas Ranger__

_____ as authorized by Chapter 181, page 444, General Laws,
Acts of Regular Session of the Forty-fourth Legislature in said State of Texas, giving and hereby granting to him all the rights, privileges, and emoluments appertaining to said appointment.

IN TESTIMONY WHEREOF, We have hereunto signed our names and caused the seal of the State of Texas, Department of Public Safety, to be affixed at the City of Austin,

the __1__ day of __January__ _____— A. D. 19.39_

Age__36__ Height__6'__ Weight__160__ Hair__Dark__ Eyes__Blue__ Complexion__Fair_

(SEAL)

M. K. Richardson
Chairman of the Public Safety Commission

G. W. Cottingham
Member of the Public Safety Commission

Albert S. Johnson
Member of the Public Safety Commission

Attested _Homer Garrison Jr_

Homer Garrison Jr
Director, Department Public Safety

This Commission expires and is void after _____ 193___

THE STATE  OF TEXAS

ADJUTANT GENERAL'S DEPARTMENT
Warrant of Authority and Descriptive List

THIS IS TO CERTIFY, That the bearer.......... Leo H. Bishop ....

is a ...... Special Ranger ...... in Company... The ... Ranger Force, State of Texas, and this is his Warrant of Authority as a Ranger, under an Act of the 36th Legislature of the State of Texas, Approved March 31, 1919, and Descriptive List for identification, and will be exhibited as his authority to Act as a Ranger when called upon for his credentials. This warrant must be surrendered to Company Commander by bearer when discharged. This Warrant of Authority and Descriptive List is signed by The Adjutant General under seal of office and attested by Company Commander.

Name	Leo H. Bishop	Rank	Special Ranger
Age	30 years 2 months	Where born	Junction, Texas
Height	5 feet 11 inches	Occupation	Ranchman
Weight	160 lbs.	Residence	Del Rio, Texas
Hair	Brown	Enlisted Where	Austin, Texas
Eyes	Blue	Enlisted When	March 27, 1933
Complexion	Fair	Enlisted by Whom	Henry Hutchings
			The Adjutant General

This warrant authority is void ... May 26, 1934

and must be returned to this Department for Cancellation.

Given under my hand and seal of office, this ...... 27th ......

day of ... March ... 193 3.

Henry Hutchings

The Adjutant General.

Attest: *R W Aldrich*

Captain Ranger Force

Commanding Co

EXECUTIVE DEPARTMENT

San Augustine native son Edward Clark was Administrative Secretary to Governor James V. Allred in Austin at the time of this letter.

C O P Y

Austin, Texas,
November 21, 1935.

Honorable Earle Thomas,
Assistant Cashier,
City National Bank,
Houston, Texas.

My dear Friend:-

The Governor is out of town on a vacation and I am therefore, unable to do anything on the Leo Bishop matter until he returns. I assure you that I will urge the Governor to station Leo permanently in San Augustine. Bishop is one of the finest and most fearless Texas rangers that ever lived. His reputation in the country where he was born and reared for honesty, integrity and bravery is one hundred percent and I am hopeful that the Governor will soon be able to get him a promotion from the rank of private.

I was glad to see you in the bank on my last visit to Houston and appreciated your courteous treatment. If I can ever serve you here, please do not hesitate to command me.

With kindest regards to yourself and wife, I remain

Your friend,

EDWARD CLARK

November 19, 1935

Honorable James V. Allred,
Governor,
State of Texas,
Austin, Texas.

Dear Governor Allred:

We have been informed that there will
be quite a few changes in the personnel of the Ranger force -
changing locations and officers. Being pretty well acquaint-
ed with the past conditions in San Augustine and knowing quite
a number of these people, I am trying to act for their good
and safety.

Leo Bishop, one of your Rangers, was
stationed there while this situation was being cleared up and
made a world of friends in the town. From what I have learned
of Mr. Bishop, he is a fine man, honest, conscientious and an
excellent peace officer. He is now stationed in Del Rio on
border patrol duty. Inasmuch as there will be a shifting of
your Ranger personnel, we would like very much to see Mr.
Bishop receive any consideration towards a promotion that you
feel he has earned.

Whatever his abilities may be, we
know the work he did in San Augustine was invaluable to the
community. The people there are very desirous of having
Mr. Bishop return to San Augustine, if it is at all possible.
I am sure that Mr. Bishop would like the move very much and believe that he could help the people of that territory with any
of their law enforcement problems that may come up.

Thanking you very much for any
consideration you may give this matter and with congratulations
on quieting down and cleaning up Texas' oldest community, I
am

Very truly yours,

H. L. Sadler,
Vice President & Trust Officer.

100

Geneva, Texas
11-6-36

State Ranger Headquarters
c/o Gov. James V. Allred
Austin, Texas

Dear Sirs:

I take this time and opportunity to express to you my sincere appreciation and gratitude for having stationed a real first class ranger in our district. Ranger Leo Bishop of whom I speak is in my estimation one of the best outstanding State Rangers that our state has employed today. We know how to value officers that will really get in behind law enforcement, because we have had so much lawlessness in our locality. Man's life was cheaper than a hog's life; the acts of certain men constituted the law of the day; women and children were constantly in open danger. Mr. Bishop is just the man to help right the lawless situation here in East Texas and help bring to the public that ray of hope for a safe environment in which man's life is more perfectly valued and protected; and where the life of all and the property of all receives the protection from the law to which it is justly entitled.

I am highly in favor of the ranger force, especially when the force is made up of men like Ranger Bishop. Texans needs more law enforcers like this gentleman. Governor, I want to personally express to you my feelings for this measure of priceless service that you have rendered to our section of the state. We want to further commend and thank you and the Department for sending to us one of the best Rangers, we think, in the entire United States.

Sincerely yours,

Rainor N. Westbrook,
Representative, 11th District.

A glowing tribute to Ranger Leo Bishop from State Representative Westbrook during Leo's first tenure here.

101

COL. H. H. CARMICHAEL
DIRECTOR

HOMER GARRISON, JR.
ASST. DIRECTOR

COMMISSION

ALBERT SIDNEY JOHNSON
CHAIRMAN

GEORGE W. COTTINGHAM

W. H. RICHARDSON, JR.
COMMISSIONERS

THE STATE OF TEXAS

DEPARTMENT OF PUBLIC SAFETY

~~AUSTIN~~

Auditorium Hotel
Houston, Texas
May 10, 1937

IN YOUR REPLY PLEASE
REFER TO FILE NO.

Mr. Leo Bishop
Texas Ranger
San Augustine, Texas

Sir:

In complying with order No. C-37, you are
hereby designated to assist in rendering
such protection and service as may be
required by President Franklin Delano
Roosevelt and his party during their stay
in the State of Texas.

You will render the above services and
act as escort for any trips the President
may care to make regardless of the Ranger
districts that may be visited.

Yours truly,

H. B. Purvis, Captain
Company A, Texas Ranger

HBP:js

H.B. Purvis, mentioned by Leo in the
interviews, was his Captain. Leo was
chosen to assist in guarding President
Franklin Delano Roosevelt during his
visit to Texas.

STATE OF TEXAS

DEPARTMENT OF PUBLIC SAFETY
AUSTIN

SPECIAL ORDERS   October 1, 1936

NO   8

      1. Leo Bishop, private, Texas Ranger, is hereby
relieved from duty with Company D, and assigned to Company A,
Texas Rangers. San Augustine, Texas, is designated as the
home station of Ranger Bishop. Ranger Bishop will report to
San Augustine for duty on or about October 10, 1936.

OFFICIAL   H. H. Carmichael,
                                                 DIRECTOR

Distribution B

Leo Bishop holding baby Babara, his wife Ruby, eldest daughter Carolyn, Gene, Bettye Sue, and Kenneth

The Stephenson home was the residence of Ranger Leo Bishop and his family during their three year tenure in San Augustine. After a short time of living in a rent-free home provided by the citizens, the Bishop family purchased this home on the corner of Milam and Hospital Streets. They sold the house in 1947, according to San Augustine County Records.

Ran

SAN AUGUSTINE RODEO

October 15 and 16

Two Shows Daily

San Augustine Fair Grounds Arena

Calf Roping, Tie-Down and Break-Away—Bronc
Riding—Bull Riding—and Bull Dogging.

Good Purses In All Events

Cowboys Grease Your Canks–Come
To this East Texas Show"

Leo Bishop, Manager

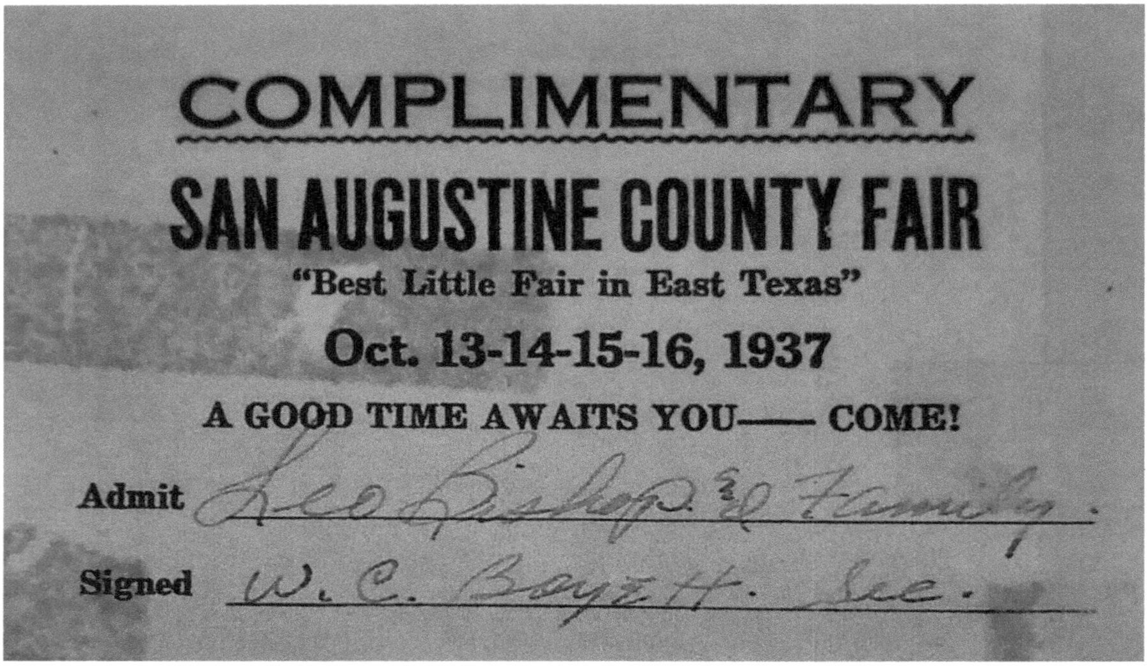

COMPLIMENTARY

SAN AUGUSTINE COUNTY FAIR

"Best Little Fair in East Texas"

Oct. 13-14-15-16, 1937

A GOOD TIME AWAITS YOU—— COME!

Admit *Leo Bishop & Family.*

Signed *W. C. Bayett. Sec.*

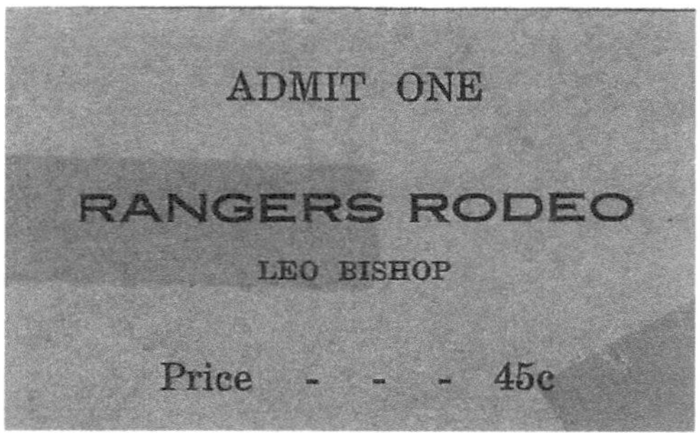

ADMIT ONE

RANGERS RODEO

LEO BISHOP

Price - - - 45c

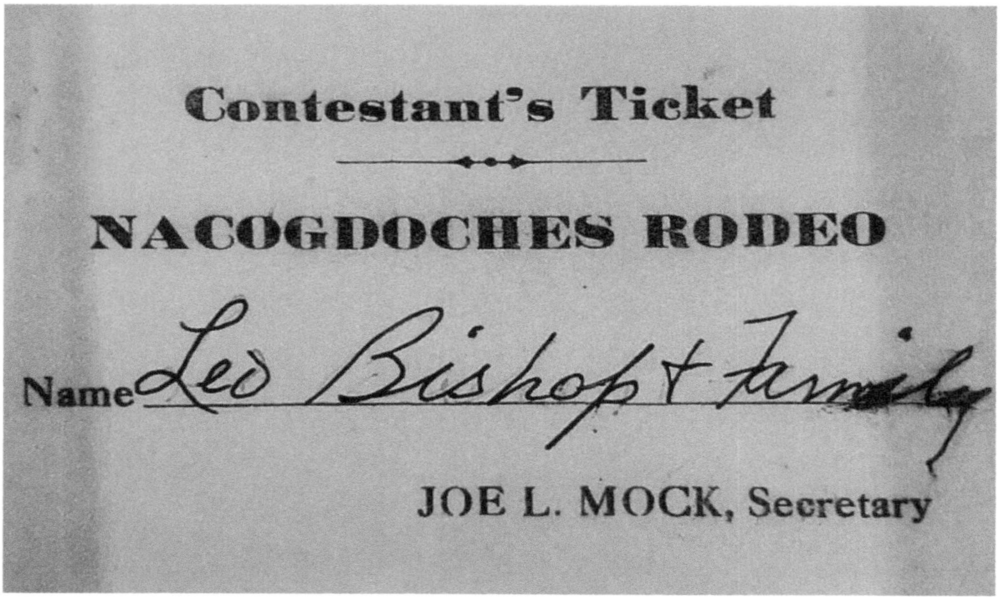

Contestant's Ticket

NACOGDOCHES RODEO

Name *Leo Bishop & Family*

JOE L. MOCK, Secretary

Ranger Bishop displaying his roping skills at his home in San Augustine

Ranger Bishop and his son Kenneth at their home in San Augustine

BLAND LAKE FISHING AND HUNTING CLUB, Inc.

J.R. GREER, PRESIDENT

W. F. HAYS, SEC.-TREAS.

SAN AUGUSTINE, TEXAS,

Apr. 29, 1939

By authority vested in me by the Board of Directors of Bland Lake Fishing & Hunting Club, Inc., I as Secretary of said club, hereby issue to

Leo Bishop, to include self and immediate family residing with him,

an Honoray fishing and hunting privilege to the said Bland Lake for the season May 1, 1939 to May 1, 1940. (It is distinctly understood that the right to carry guests is not included.)

Signed *W F Hays*

Secretary Bland Lake F. & H. Club, Inc.

Boat House at Bland Lake, Texas.

Bland Lake was created by the Bland family in the 1890s from a dam built on the Ayish Bayou to power their sawmill. A gristmill for grinding corn was constructed on the lake a few years later. By 1902 survey crews had placed the tracks for the new railroad next to Bland Lake. Jeff Bland constructed a bath house, dance pavilion, and covered picnic areas at the site for recreational purposes. A sixty-foot-high slide, called a "chute-de-chute," was built on the lake for the swimmers. Fishing memberships and season tickets for using Bland Lake were enjoyed by San Augustine County citizens. Ranger Leo Bishop and his family were given free privileges there during their years in San Augustine. In recent years the gas well in the Bland Lake vicinity was named in honor of Ranger Leo Bishop, the "Bishop #1."

Bland Lake dance pavilion, bath house and covered picnic area. (top)

"chute-de-chute" waterslide - Bland Lake, Texas (bottom)

St. Mary Land &
Exploration Company

BISHOP 1-H
RRC ID 263851
797.988 ACRES
LAT 31.5777270°N
LON 94.1285144°W

Robert Kilpatrick of St. Mary Land & Exploration Company came to San Augustine to set up locations in the Haynesville Shale. He had an affinity for historical figures and named the gas and oil wells for different explorers, adventurers and lawmen. He named the BISHOP 1-H location (northeast of town) after legendary Leo Bishop...the much loved (by the citizens of San Augustine) Texas Ranger.

The BISHOP 1-H is in the Bland Lake community where Leo spent time fishing, swimming and spending time with family and friends.

It is a reminder to this day of Leo's service to San Augustine County and is now operated by Aethon Energy .

San Augustine High School. (top) Leo's eldest daughter Carolyn graduated from there in 1939. Birth of a baby boy, Frank Lloyd Dent into a well-known San Augustine Family. (bottom)

Hello Ranger Bishop:

Dad says you live just back of us and I am anxious to meet you. It was mighty fine of you to send me that gun. Dad said something about burglars and kidnappers living in this big strange world into which I have come. Well, thanks to you I am prepared for them now. But my big problem is going to be keeping dad from wearing out my gun until I get a chance to crack down on one of those nannies.

Thanks a lot Ranger. If you ever need any possemen you know where I live.   Frank Lloyd Dent.   My X. mark.

Kenneth and Gene Bishop (Leo and Ruby's sons)

Pictured at the family home during their three-year stay in San Augustine, Texas

Ruby with her daughters Carolyn (L) and Bettye (r)

**Photo is from the 1940s, after the family moved back to the
Carta Valley area of South Texas.**

RANGER BISHOP SECURES CONFESSION OF UNTAX-PAID GAS "RUNNERS" JAILED HERE

Friday Ranger Leo Bishop's telephone rang and information was conveyed to him that the Comptroller's Department Field office in the Rusk County oil field was having trouble with untax-paid gasoline runners and that Tully Scott, State Officer, would call on him with full details and asking aid, which Bishop readily assured would be forthcoming. Just how complete and such a "nice feather", so to speak, for his own cap Ranger Bishop did not of course realize in the beginning. The information given him was that a truck with gasoline and manifest calling for 1,022 gallons and tax paid on that amount had been seized near Arp. The operator of the truck, B. T. Townsend of Zavalla, was arrested, but permitted to phone to his home to bring a car for him. While preliminaries were being attended to the truck with contents disappeared from the highway. Ranger Leo Bishop aided two State officers in the Comptroller's Department and went to Zavalla where upon thorough investigation the following were arrested and confined in jail here Friday evening: Henry Townsend, and two sons, B. T. and T. H. Townsend, according to Ranger Bishop who state that three felony charges were filed against each party

Saturday in Travis County, Texas. The investigation resulted in signed confessions of Henry Townsend and son, T. H., that the truck with gasoline was driven away from the scene near Arp, brought to the Zavalla section where the Townsends operate a string of service stations under the name of the Townsend Oil Co. and gas removed from tank and truck driven to Houston where a false tank inside the cylindrical drum with a capacity of 150 gallons was plugged and the truck left parked in a prominent place in that city. Ranger Bishop stated that it was a very clever arrangement and such practices had given the Comptroller's Department considerable trouble and that he was happy to be of assistance in this instance.

Considerable argument took place over the matter prior to the confession and B. T. Townsend was most abusive, according to the State Ranger, finally making fight on him, which necessitated the use of his six-gun as a club, Bishop stated. His wound was dressed in a local physician's office here late Friday. The Townsends were released on bond late Saturday. Attorney J. R. Bogard has been retained to represent them in the Travis County District Court.

120

Two Rangers

This interesting image from the Leo Bishop memoirs of Family Historian Bettye Bishop Robbins shows Texas Ranger Leo Bishop in his familiar pose with one foot on the Car's running board. His traveling companion, although unnamed, is likely a friend and law enforcement officer who assisted him during his three-year return to San Augustine in 1936. The handwritten caption under the photo, "Two Rangers," is descriptive of the camaraderie enjoyed between the men working together in keeping the peace.

TWO TALES ABOUT TEXAS RANGER LEO BISHOP

Author Larry Trekell was employed by the United States Forest Service for many years in the Forest Trail Region of East Texas. He worked on land appraisals for the Forest Service, and had ample opportunity to visit with many local citizens and hear their stories. The following two episodes relating to Texas Ranger Leo Bishop are used with the permission of author Trekell, who interestingly recorded the stories in the vernacular of those who told them to him.

An Account from Tom Gilliam to Larry Trekell:

Livestock owners in Texas were ordered to dip livestock for the Texas cattle fever tick eradication program in the early 1930s, and Hector Pilot, a leader in the East Hamilton community of Shelby County, refused to dip. He distrusted the "guvvamint: as much as anyone did, viewing this as just another strong-arm boondoggle on their part.

The Shelby County Agent had hired Tom Gilliam as an aide-de-camp in the presentation and enforcement of the dipping orders, and Tom was having all kinds of trouble with "Heck," so he enlisted the aid of Texas Ranger Leo Bishop. Ranger Bishop, according to those who knew him, was a legend in his own time. He was a man who wore little round wire-framed spectacles and a matched pair of pearl-handled Colt .44 revolvers. The number of men he'd had to face down was large, but probably grew in the telling. He had been sent to San Augustine to "clean up" the feuding and killing in the late 1920s and early 1930s, which is a whole 'nuther story. Tom and Ranger Bishop went out to Heck's house, approached the front

Stomp, hollered, "Hello, the house!" and waited. Heck came to the door, and ranger Bishop announced who they were and what they came about.

In those days, more often than not, country folks had a shotgun on two big nails above the front door. As they talked, Heck's hands moved to the door facings, and began to "inch" upward a little at a time. This is the way Tom Gilliam related the story to me: "Ranger Bishop was in mid-sentence, a'telling' Heck he wuz a'gonta hafta dip, when, without breakin' stride, he sez, 'Heck, move yore hands up th' door facin's one more inch, an' yore a dead man!' then went right on a'talkin' an' Heck never moved 'em again neither! He knowed better! Thet 'uz Leo Bishop he 'uz a'foolin' with!"

An Account from Jeff Scarbrough to Larry Trekell:

"My daddy-in-law Mr. Vestal Metcalf was sot in his ways, now! He didn't do nuthin' 'til Mr. Metcalf got ready! I 'member one time th' govvamint came out to git 'im to move a fence he had over the line a little on the forest land. He tells 'em he'll move it when it needs rebuildin', and not before. Well-sir, hit ain't long 'til Leo Bishop comes out an' tells 'im, he sez, 'Mr. Metcalf, I come out to tell ya to move yer fence ta th' line, an' I'm givin' ya ten days to git er done.' Mr. Bishop, he ain't no big imposing' feller. Little sandy-haired feller, weigh about a hunnert an' fifty pound. Wore a six-gun on both sides. Mr. Vestal, he sez, 'Maybe I'll move 'er when the posts git rotten.' I sez, 'Mr. Vestal, Do you know who you're a'talkin' to like that? That's Leo Bishop, the man that cleaned up San Augustine. You better pay some attention to him, now!'

Well, Bishop, he sez, 'Mr. Metcalf, I'm a'comin' back out here in ten days, an' you better be done with that fence movin', an' if you wanta object enny more, that ten days is a'gonna shrink to five!' an' he left. Well, sir, that's one time Mr. Vestal did something' afore he got ready! 'Bout three days later...he hadn't said much one way 'er t'other 'bout that fence...he sez, 'Boys, let's go split some posts.' Am' we did. Had that fence back on line in five days!

(A group of 30 citizens went to Austin to request the return of Ranger Leo Bishop to be stationed permanently in San Augustine. He stayed three years, from 1936-1939. the following article appeared in the San Augustine Tribune.)

Citizens Showing Their Appreciation of Bishop

Another instance of appreciation upon the part of the citizenship of San Augustine County for the stationing permanently here of State Ranger Leo Bishop came to light when it became known that citizens contributed money for a fine pair of ivory handles for his six-guns. They are embellished with longhorn steer heads and lend a wild west appearance to these beautiful guns. A nice suit of clothes was also given to the Ranger by the well-known firm of A.J. Wood and Bros. with Mr. W.P. Wood making the presentation. Such hearty consideration and genuine appreciation of the splendid officer shows conclusively that the leading citizens of the city re awakening to law enforcement.

"I want you to really thank those people...I just can't find words to express my feelings," said Ranger Bishop to a Tribune reporter Monday while telling us of his honors above mentioned. It's a hard thing to do. In fact, mere words are inadequate to the situation, but when one can see the gleam of satisfaction and appreciation wreathed all over the face of this good-looking Ranger it's easy to realize that he means every word of it, and he will just have to live his appreciation, and we are a assured of that in the beginning.

That's no doubt one of the reasons why everyone is so nice to Bishop. All realize that there is no camouflage about him-that he is indeed earnest on the job he was sent to complete, that of seeing that law and order prevail in San Augustine County.

The March 28, 1935 edition of the 𝕾𝖆𝖓 𝕬𝖚𝖌𝖚𝖘𝖙𝖎𝖓𝖊 𝕿𝖗𝖎𝖇𝖚𝖓𝖊 :

An excellent first-hand account of the crucial role played by the Texas Rangers in bringing a quick conclusion to the San Augustine crime wave that beset this East Texas area for several prior years. 𝕿𝖗𝖎𝖇𝖚𝖓𝖊 Publisher-Editor Webster F. Hays was both courageous and informative in describing to his readers the events and details of those tumultuous days as they happened. His narrative from the front page is presented in a larger, more readable font and includes the continued story from page 8 of the March 28, 1935 edition.

Telegram From Governor Allred

Austin, Texas, March 25.

W. F. Hays,
San Augustine Tribune,
San Augustine, Texas.

The fine spirit of good citizenship which the people of San Augustine County have shown in approving the action of the Texas Rangers is gratifying, indeed, to the Governor of your State. Your street dance celebration honoring the Rangers is indicative of a healthy public sentiment which will not tolerate vicious, violent lawlessness. With the powerful force of public approval behind them local officers throughout the State cannot fail in their efforts to enforce the laws. As Governor of Texas I heartily commend your action and promise you my continued efforts to rid the State of lawlessness.

JAMES V. ALLRED,
Governor of Texas.

San Augustine Tribune.

NEW ERA   NEW ERA

VOL. XXVII.   SAN AUGUSTINE, TEXAS.   THURSDAY, MARCH 28, 1935.   NUMBER 1

APPROVE RULE OF RANGERS

4,000 People Gather for Big Street Dance Celebrating General Clean-Up

Friday night was a gala occasion for San Augustine. As previously advertised throughout this entire section by circulars and in these columns a big street dance was held honoring the Rangers and in general celebration over the New Era, that of law enforcement, in San Augustine County.

A block in the main street was roped-off and with a dance orchestra from the Stephen F. Austin College, Nacogdoches, furnishing music the big free dance was on. Constable H.S. Sharp* called the meeting to order and introduced Hon. J.R. Bogard*, who introduced Ranger Captain J. W. McCormick and Ranger Leo Bishop, who gratefully acknowledged the introduction and prolonged hand-clapping of approval by the large crowd. Captain McCormick and Mrs. Herman D. Clark* and Ranger Leo Bishop and Mrs. J.H. Ellington* led the first dance, which was quickly joined by hundreds of couples.

Attorney Bogard in his introduction of the Rangers stated that this occasion was arranged to honor the Rangers for their service to San Augustine County citizens in cleaning-up unlawful conditions, to cement a stronger friendship between the people of San Augustine and its trade territory and for a better feeling among us all.

The large crowd was composed of citizens, both men and women, from practically every nook and corner of the county and other nearby sections, all rejoicing over improved conditions here.

Mr. Raymond Allred, brother of Governor James V. Allred, came from Wichita Falls to represent the governor upon this occasion. The protection offered San Augustine County direct from the Governor is a part of the law enforcement program of the Governor throughout the State. We quote from Friday's papers:

Austin, March 22: "Governor James V. Allred declared Friday that 'there will be no quarter' in the fight on open gambling and saloons in Texas. He reiterated that the present drive of the Rangers is a war between open gambling houses and open saloons on the one side and law and order on the other."

Joints formerly dispensing liquor on the main street of San Augustine have long since ceased and raids by *(page 8 of Tribune begins here)* Rangers have netted considerable bottled-in-bond stocks and it has gotten so scarce here that no evidence whatsoever of drinking was to be seen at the street dance Friday night.

The crowd frolicked in free abandon until the wee small hours of the night. Sentiment for law enforcement is growing by leaps and bounds, due to the positive enforcement program of the

Rangers, assisted by local elected officers. Former officials had completely "layed-down" on the job and misdirected authority had prevailed until conditions had grown well nigh intolerable. The citizenship has been assured that the next few months will be the completion of the job the Rangers have begun. More power to their strong arm is the uttered and unexpected sentiment of the general citizenship.

It is fitting indeed, and quite appropriate that San Augustine should celebrate in open Street Dance. It would not be out of order if this kind of celebration should be held once each month. Upon such an occasion the people of the surrounding country could be invited guests and see for themselves that a New Era is in progress here.

H.S. Sharp became Sheriff of San Augustine County soon afterward.

Mrs. Herman D. Clark ("Miss Exa," sister-in-law of Edward Clark) and Mrs. J.H. Ellington (Verna, wife of local family physician Dr. Ellington) were among a number of San Augustine County women who were active in community affairs and worthy causes.

J.R. Bogard was a noted attorney in San Augustine County, grandfather of Sharon Bogard Bradberry and former County Judge Jack Nichols.

To the Citizenship of San Augustine County:

With a feeling of pride in your approval we greet you. The expression of confidence accorded us last Friday evening warms our heart with gratitude and we are glad, indeed, to be here to serve a people who respond so readily to leadership.

In this connection we desire to say that when our final report has been made to the Governor on conditions in San Augustine County we unhesitatingly assure you that it will be complete in every detail and that law and order will prevail here as it should.

We will be pleased to have the co-operation of the general public and again thank you for the splendid demonstration and honor in our behalf upon this occasion.

Respectfully,

CAPT. J. W. McCORMICK

LAW ENFORCEMENT GOES MERRILY ON

A still was seized last week as the property of Frank Teel, 10 gallons of home brew and 100 gallons of "buck" destroyed by Constable Sharp and Chief Jones.

Isaac Roberts was taken into custody and place in jail Friday by Constable Sharp, Ranger Bishop and Chief of Police Jones, charged with selling intoxicating liquor.

LEO BISHOP'S

LATER DAYS IN

SOUTH TEXAS

(l-r) Ernest Best, Zeno Smith, Jim Flournoy and Leo Bishop at Big Bend, 1940. 40 miles up river from Presidio

NOW IT'S HI-YO SILVER IN A HORSEMOBILE!

ANGERS PETE CRAWFORD (LEFT) AND LEO BISHOP ARE SHOWN WITH TRAILER FOR MOUNTS.
Nags are moved in trailer via streamlining until going gets rough; then horse comes into its own.

Texas Rangers Pete Crawford (left) and Leo Bishop pose beside their "Horsemobile" during the early 1940s, after Leo and his family moved from San Augustine. Locale in the photo was South Texas.

Leo Bishop and Pete Crawford on Patrol near Mexican Border

On the border between Texas and Mexico, Captain Ernest Best,

Jim Flournoy, Leo Bishop, Pete Crawford. 1943

Leo and friends in South Texas after returning from his years in San Augustine.

Leo Bishop and Pete Crawford at Big Bend, about 20 miles below Boquillas, 1940

Ranger Who Cleaned Up Crime Now Ranchman

ALPINE, Tex., June 14. —One of the most typical members of the Texas Rangers has resigned to go into ranch work in the Big Bend of Texas. He is Leo Bishop, who was born at Junction in 1903 and entered the Ranger service at Del Rio in 1932. His first big chance came in 1935 when he was sent by Gov. Allred to San Augustine to clear up a situation that had developed there. In 90 days Bishop had turned in 19 indictments for murder and all of the defendants got sentences from 1 to 99 years. Later, Bishop was honored a a banquet in Beaumont by Gov. Allred, and still later, 30 leading citizens of San Augustine made a trip to Austin and requested the governor to station Bishop there permanently.

During his 12 years in the service, Bishop has led to the conviction of more than 100 major criminals. Less than a year ago, he prepared evidence that produced the only death sentence ever given in Jeff Davis County.

While in the Ranger service, Bishop has been stationed at Del Rio twice, San Augustine twice, Hebbronville, Uvalde, Eagle Pass, and Alpine.

A good ranch hand, Bishop was often found riding with cowhands helping them with their work while at the same time collecting evidence. Most of the rodeos in the area where he was stationed found him competing with and often winning from the best calf ropers in the country.

From the Bettye Bishop Robbins Family Collection.

Carta Valley Ranch Home of Leo and Ruby Bishop.

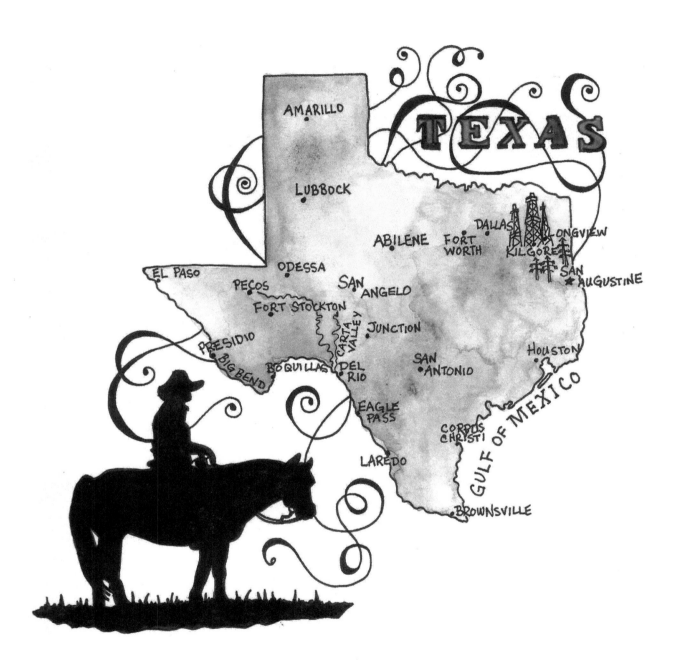

AUTOGRAPH RANGER BOOK - Dr. Ben Proctor, seated, talks with Gladys Woods, widow of a former San Augustine law man, Ken Woods, after autographing his new book, "Just One Riot—Episodes of the Texas Rangers in the the 20th Century." In the background are three ex and present Rangers, N.W. Dub Clark, L.T. Carpenter, Maurice Cook of Austin, active Senior Ranger Captain, Willie Earl Tindall, Historian, Bettye Bishop Robbins, daughter of Famed Texas Ranger Leo Bishop, who lived in San Augustine for several years.

Photo by: San Augustine Tribune

**Leo and Ruby Bishop celebrating 25 years of marriage
in this photo**

COUPLE WED 50 YEARS HONORED AT BARBECUE

MR. & MRS. LEO BISHOP

Approximately 100 friends from Alpine, points in Texas and out-of-state attended the barbecue dinner Saturday, Feb 20,1971 honoring Mr. and Mrs. Leo Bishop, on their 50th wedding anniversary.

The barbecue which started at 11a.m. and continued throughout the day was held at the Carta Valley ranch home of Mr. and Mrs. Bishop.

Hosts were the couple's children and families: Mr. and Mrs. Grady Nelon of Alpine, Kenneth Bishop of Del Rio, Mr. and Mrs. D.J. Robbins of Houston, Mr. and Mrs. Bill Savell of Sonora and Gene Bishop of Carta Valley.

Mr. and Mrs. Bishop were married Feb. 16, 1921 only 10 miles from where the celebration was held. The young couple had heard that an old-fashioned "shivaree" was being planned for them at the time and place of their wedding so they decided to exchange vows in a Hudson car with the Baptist preacher and their attendants.

Adding to a special note of pleasure to the affair was the presence of 5 generations through the 5 children of the honorees, Mrs. Nelon, and her brother, Gene Bishop, Mrs. Nelon's daughter, Carol Ann (Mrs. Bill) Spears and her baby daughter, Barbara Diane of Houston and Gene Bishop and his daughter, Carol Gene (Mrs. Rodney) Cottle and her 2 children, and Mrs. Buck Bishop (Allene) of Rock Springs, mother of Leo, rounded out the 5 generations.

Mr. and Mrs. Bishop have 11 grandchildren and 5 great-grandchildren.

Rites For Leo Bishop Held Friday

(Obituary from the Sonora, Texas newspaper)

Services for Mr. Leo H. Bishop, 70, were held Friday morning at First Baptist Church. The Rev. Clifton Hancock, pastor, officiated at the services. Burial was in Carta Valley Cemetery at 2 p.m.

Mr. Bishop died September 25, 1973 at his ranch home east of Carta Valley after suffering a heart attack.

He was born January 15, 1903 in Junction and served with the Texas Rangers for fourteen years. He was a special ranger in Sonora from 1953-1959 and was in the ranching profession in Carta Valley at the time of his death.

Married to Ruby Nation, February 16, 1921, he and Mrs. Bishop celebrated their 50th anniversary in 1971. He was a member of the Baptist Church of Sonora.

Survivors include his wife; two sons, Gene Bishop of Carta Valley, and Kenneth Bishop of Del Rio; three daughters, Mrs. Grady Nelon of Alpine, Mrs. D.J. Robbins of Houston and Mrs. Bill Savell; his mother, Mrs. Allene Bishop of Rocksprings; three brothers, Teil Bishop and Ned Bishop of Carta Valley and J.C. Bishop of Dallas; 11 grandchildren and six great-grandchildren.

Pallbearers were L.H. Purvis of Kerrville, Ervin Willman, Joe Felps of Junction, John R. Riggs of Del Rio, Stillman Long of Del Rio, Cecil Chrane of San Antonio and John Harrison of Dryden.

Serving as honorary pallbearers were all his friends and old law enforcement officers of Texas.

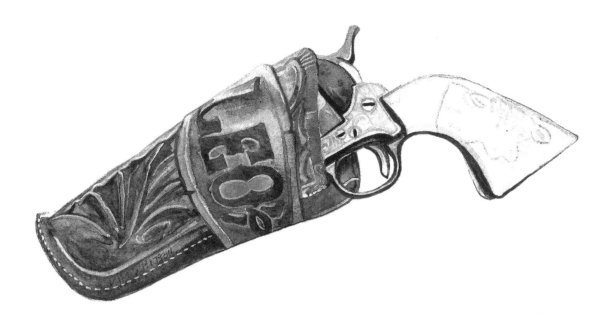

THE FIRST TEXAS RANGERS

**In 1823, Stephen F. Austin commissioned
10 lawmen to keep the peace in
Texas' First American Settlement
and called them "Rangers."**

**By 1826, representatives of Austin's
six districts
came together and agreed to keep
"Twenty or Thirty Rangers in service."**

**At a Consultation of Texas leaders
at San Felipe de Austin on
October 17, 1835,
a corps of Rangers was officially created.**